COMPACT

FIRST
FOR SCHOOLS
THIRD EDITION

B2
WORKBOOK
WITHOUT ANSWERS
WITH EBOOK

Joanna Kosta

Shaftesbury Road, Cambridge CB2 8EA, United Kingdom

One Liberty Plaza, 20th Floor, New York, NY 10006, USA

477 Williamstown Road, Port Melbourne, VIC 3207, Australia

314–321, 3rd Floor, Plot 3, Splendor Forum, Jasola District Centre, New Delhi – 110025, India

103 Penang Road, #05–06/07, Visioncrest Commercial, Singapore 238467

Cambridge University Press & Assessment is a department of the University of Cambridge.

We share the University's mission to contribute to society through the pursuit of education, learning and research at the highest international levels of excellence.

www.cambridge.org
Information on this title: www.cambridge.org/9781009167222

First published 2013
Second edition 2014
Third edition 2023

20 19 18 17 16 15 14 13 12 11 10 9 8 7 6 5

Printed in Great Britain by CPI Group (UK) Ltd, Croydon CR0 4YY

A catalogue record for this publication is available from the British Library

ISBN   978-1-009-16722-2   Workbook without answers with eBook

Additional resources for this publication at www.cambridge.org/compact

Contents

1 My community

Listening

Part 3

1 What can people do to make new friends? Write three suggestions to add to A–H in the exam task below.

Need help? Go to Exam tips page 6 in the Student's Book

✓ Exam task

🔊 **02** You will hear five short extracts in which teenagers are talking about making new friends. For questions **1–5**, choose from the list (**A–H**) what each speaker says. Use the letters only once. There are three extra letters which you do not need to use.

A show that you are willing to help

B present yourself as you really are

C highlight an interest you have in common

D invite people to do things with you

E hide any anxiety you are feeling

F pay close attention when people talk to you

G don't expect friendships to develop quickly

H be as funny as you can

Speaker 1 **1** ☐

Speaker 2 **2** ☐

Speaker 3 **3** ☐

Speaker 4 **4** ☐

Speaker 5 **5** ☐

Grammar

Present and future tenses

1 Choose the correct words to complete each sentence.

1 **I have** / **I'll have** a piano lesson every Saturday morning. I have done since I was five.

2 **I'll call** / **I'm calling** you as soon as I've finished my breakfast.

3 It's 8.30 already! **You're being** / **You're going to be** late!

4 I can't play tennis with you because **I'm going** / **I go** to the dentist later.

5 I can't wait! This time tomorrow **I'll be lying** / **I'm lying** on a beach in Spain!

6 I understand what you're saying, but **I'm not agreeing** / **I don't agree** with you.

7 I can't spend any more money this month. **I'm saving** / **I'll save** up for a car.

8 Children **are loving** / **love** sweet things much more than adults.

9 **I'm going to make** / **I'm making** a real effort to work harder next term so I pass my exam.

10 **I'll fix** / **I'm fixing** your bike before I go to the football match this afternoon.

Vocabulary

Relationships

1 Complete each sentence with a word from the box.

after	in	off	on	out	to	with

1 Jessica and I hit it .... the first time we met – we've got similar ideas about everything.

2 My sister, who takes .... my mum, is tall and fair.

3 I fell .... with my best friend because she copied from me in a test.

4 My brother has been going out .... his girlfriend for two years now.

5 I get .... well with my younger brother, but not with my older one.

6 It took me a long time to get .... know Claire because she's really quiet.

7 My uncle always says he fell .... love with my aunt the moment he first saw her.

Reading and Use of English

Part 5

1 Read the text opposite quickly and answer the questions.

1 What's the topic of the text?
2 What type of text is it?
3 What is the writer doing in the text?

Need help? Go to Exam tip page 10 in the Student's Book

✓ Exam task

You are going to read a blog post about writing to pen pals. For questions **1–3**, choose the best answer (**A**, **B**, **C** or **D**) which you think fits best according to the text.

1 What does the writer suggest about the relationship she had with her first pen pal?
  A It was disappointingly brief.
  B It made a strong impression on her.
  C Its importance to her grew as time went by.
  D It changed when they began writing to each other.

2 The writer uses the verb 'dash off' in line 17 to suggest that
  A people have to deal with a lot of emails.
  B people use a casual writing style in emails.
  C little effort goes into writing emails.
  D email replaced letter-writing very suddenly.

3 From the final paragraph we understand that the writer thinks it isn't necessary to
  A have any particular aim when you write letters.
  B make the letters you send look decorative.
  C meet up with pen pals if you prefer not to.
  D stick to conventional choices of pen pal.

The joy of having a pen pal

My name's Anna, I'm 17 years old and I love writing letters. In this blog post I'm going to try to explain what the attraction is.

For me, the words 'pen pal' take me right back to a wonderful summer holiday I had in Spain, when I was about ten. I spent the days swimming and chatting with my new friend, Toni. After the holiday we kept in touch by letter – I can't recall how long for. But what's still fresh in my mind is how it felt to make a connection with another person. And then, once we started corresponding, how it felt to go through the morning post and find, amongst all the advertising leaflets and bills for my parents, an actual handwritten letter in an envelope.

I know the idea of writing letters seems terribly old-fashioned to most people. There doesn't seem much point when we can just follow each other on social media. If we want to write, we're much more likely to exchange emails than put pen to paper. Emails are invaluable and I wouldn't be without them, but they're something you just dash off. It's not like a letter that demands time and effort to put together. Phone calls are great too, but you can't hold them afterwards, or carry them around with you.

According to most people's definition, a pen pal is someone you write to, but don't see in person. However, I wouldn't be quite so strict about it. It's perfectly possible to pick someone in your family to be pen pals with, for example. At the moment I'm exchanging letters with my nephew who's recently started school. He gets to practise his writing skills and I love finding out what he's been up to. He always covers his envelope with stickers and drawings, and I sometimes include a little gift with my letter.

Vocabulary

Words with similar meanings

1 Complete the sentences with the correct word.

1 This area can .... flooded very quickly if there's heavy rain. **occur / become**

2 The sun might come out later, but I think it's .... unlikely. **highly / widely**

3 My attempt at painting a tree didn't .... the result I was hoping for. **produce / involve**

4 Jake, your piano playing has improved .... this term. **deeply / greatly**

5 Jane was in the water for so long she .... blue. **turned / changed**

6 Completing the project on time .... difficult. **confirmed / proved**

7 Success is often put down to hard work, but luck can .... a part too. **make / play**

8 My grandparents are still .... in love after 50 years of marriage. **highly / deeply**

9 TV game shows often .... answering questions or solving puzzles. **make / involve**

10 The article was so hard to understand – I couldn't .... sense of it. **produce / make**

11 Please .... seated until the plane stops completely. **remain / continue**

12 The novel is .... thought to be the author's best work. **widely / greatly**

2 Complete each sentence with a quantity or amount word from the box. Think about collocation, grammar and meaning when making your choice. There are six words you don't need.

> degree   dimension   extent   increase   majority
> minority   percentage   quantity   sample   scale

1 The .... in the number of students attending after-school clubs was unexpected.

2 The full .... of the problem wasn't understood at first.

3 To succeed at horse riding you need a high .... of skill.

4 A very low .... of students are brought to school by car.

Grammar

Comparisons

1 Complete the sentences with one word.

1 I get on better with my younger sister .... my older one.

2 The more I read about the Ancient Egyptians, ... more interested I got.

3 I'm not .... good at French as I'd like to be.

4 The more time I spend on this project, the .... time I have for my hobbies.

5 The sunglasses cost .... than I could afford.

6 My parents would always prefer .... go camping rather than stay in a hotel.

7 This beach is .... good as the one we usually go to.

8 The longer I had to wait for my results, the .... nervous I became.

9 My brother enjoys school a .... more than I do.

10 Skiing is impossible this year because there's far .... snow than usual.

Reading and Use of English

Part 1

Need help? Go to Exam tip page 7 in the Student's Book

✓ Exam task

For questions **1–8**, read the text below and decide which answer (**A**, **B**, **C** or **D**) best fits each gap.
There is an example at the beginning (**0**).

Example: 0   **A** underestimated   **B** distracted   **C** undone   **D** discouraged

1 A gather	**B** collect	**C** reach	**D** combine
2 A provided	**B** contributed	**C** donated	**D** supplied
3 A related	**B** tied	**C** associated	**D** paired
4 A involve	**B** contain	**C** demand	**D** expect
5 A bringing up	**B** putting down	**C** following up	**D** carrying out
6 A favour	**B** touch	**C** view	**D** progress
7 A firmly	**B** slightly	**C** relatively	**D** rapidly
8 A force	**B** impact	**C** result	**D** consequence

Why festivals matter

The importance of festivals to culture and society should not be **(0)** ....A......... . At these events, large numbers of people from all sorts of backgrounds **(1)** .... together to celebrate, leaving the stresses of everyday life behind them.

Historical events, religion and local legends have all significantly **(2)** .... to the tradition of festivals. Agriculture is important too – many festivals are **(3)** .... with the time of harvest. In some parts of the world, festivals **(4)** ....

the sharing of stories and experiences by community elders. By **(5)** .... this task, the older generation is able to keep younger generations in **(6)** .... with their traditions.

More modern types of festivals include book festivals, food festivals and wellness festivals. A **(7)** .... new type of festival that has had a big **(8)** .... on the cultural lives of young people is the music festival. There are now hundreds of these around the world and the number is growing all the time.

Home and away

Reading and Use of English

1 Read the text below about the purpose of adventure. What type of text is it? Where would you read it?

Need help? Go to Exam tip page 14 in the Student's Book

✓ Exam task

You are going to read an article about the purpose of adventure. Six sentences have been removed from the article. Choose from the sentences **A–G** the one which fits each gap (**1–6**). There is one extra sentence which you do not need to use.

The purpose of adventure in the 21st century

In every era of history, adventurers and explorers have ventured out into the wild and unmapped parts of our planet. Some, like Charles Darwin, went with the aim of making new scientific discoveries. Others, such as the British polar explorer Ernest Shackleton, seem to have been motivated by the desire to push themselves and test the limits of their capabilities. This seems to be what drives a lot of modern adventurers, but some are beginning to question whether this is valid any more, given the problems facing our planet.

Sal Montgomery is an adventure kayak guide and is often seen on TV, leading expeditions along remote rivers in places like Bhutan, or the Kamchatka peninsula in Russia. She is a supporter of the idea of 'purposeful adventure' and points out that until recently, the way adventurers were shown on TV was all about the individual.

(1) .... This approach, she believes, is changing rapidly. Audiences now want to know what the meaning behind a trip is, and what good will come out of it.

Montgomery creates meaning not only by highlighting the state of the natural world when on an expedition – but by attempting to make up for any harm her trip might have caused once she gets back. **(2)** .... Her efforts raised a significant sum for the rainforest-conservation charity, the World Land Trust.

Montgomery also makes a point of highlighting the importance of inspiring young people, and regularly visits schools to talk about her work. She believes passionately that the barriers that prevent access to nature need to come down. **(3)** .... People will care enough to want to do it on their own.

Of course, our ability to push into the remote corners of our planet has increased dramatically since the days of Shackleton. Technological advances mean that expeditions today are cheaper but far more carbon intensive than ever before. **(4)** .... These are people who love the planet and want to dedicate their lives to exploring it, but doing so leads them to damage it.

Some say that the age of exploration is over, as the unmapped regions of the planet have gone from entire continents to a few mountaintops. This does make being 'first' to anywhere pretty difficult, but maybe climate change gives adventurers an opportunity. **(5)** .... Their role can be to communicate this to the rest of us.

A certain celebrity is still attached to the people who return from our remaining wild places. **(6)** .... It seems we no longer want explorers who come back from the wilderness with a story about themselves. We want to hear about our planet.

Listening

1 Read through the context sentences. Which do you think will be monologues and which will be dialogues?

Need help? Go to Exam tip page 69 in the Student's Book

✓ Exam task

🔊 **03** You will hear people talking in six different situations. For questions **1–6**, choose the best answer (**A**, **B** or **C**).

1 You hear a boy talking about a computer course he did during his summer holiday.
What does he say about it?
A It's not clear why his dad selected it.
B He hesitated before agreeing to it.
C Overall it was a positive experience.

2 You hear two friends talking about a podcast series.
What do they agree about the choice of topics?
A Most aren't relevant to teenagers.
B They're not the reason for listening.
C It's surprising how interesting they are.

3 You hear a report on the radio about an expedition.
What information is being kept a secret for now?
A what the mountain is called
B when the expedition will take place
C which type of bikes will be used

4 You hear a girl talking to her father about a problem she's got.
How is the girl feeling?
A uncertain about what to do next
B impatient about her lack of progress in something
C hopeful that a solution has been found

5 You hear a teenager talking to his grandmother about his recent move.
What does he say about it?
A He appreciates how convenient his new location is.
B He's ready to start making new friends.
C He's pleased with how quickly he's adjusted.

6 You hear part of a class debate.
What is the girl doing?
A questioning the need for a new statue
B complaining about the style of the new statue
C offering her support for the new statue

A However, our judgement of what they are doing there appears to be becoming sharper.
B Once that happens, it will no longer be necessary to make the case for looking after our wild places.
C Indeed, it's not clear exactly what expectations we should have of them.
D In one case, this involved taking two months off work in order to go on a lecture tour of the UK.
E By visiting remote regions – the rainforests, a desert, the Arctic or Antarctic – they get a clear view of its impact.
F Some guy was seen flying around the world, going to remote locations just to show off how tough he was.
G As a result, many adventurers now face a dilemma.

2 Read the audio script on page 44 and underline the words that gave you the answer to each question.

Grammar

used to and would

1 Complete the sentences with *used to* or *would*. Sometimes both are possible, and sometimes you need the negative form.

1 Your teacher .... give you more homework than he does now, didn't he?
2 Before we moved into this house, we .... live in an apartment.
3 When she was little, Tania .... eat an egg for breakfast every day.
4 I .... like going for walks when I was young, but I love it now.
5 When I was little, my mum .... sing to me at bedtime.
6 Nicky .... be able to speak French, but he's forgotten most of it now.
7 My brother .... be very sporty when he was little, but he prefers video games now.
8 I don't watch a lot of TV any more, but I ....

Past tenses

2 Complete the sentences by choosing the correct verb form.

1 There **was being** / **was** a big demonstration through the town centre at 1 p.m.
2 It's been a long time since I **swam** / **had swum** in the ocean.
3 Since my brother started learning the violin, we **had had** / **have had** no peace at home!
4 When I lived in Japan, I **made** / **was making** lots of friends.
5 By the time Jen asked me to join her band, I **'d already formed** / **have already formed** my own.
6 My grandparents **were sitting** / **had sat** in their living room when the storm began.
7 I **was** / **'ve been** interested in history since I was at primary school.
8 My sister **'s been working** / **worked** as a lawyer for two years after she finished university.

Adverb formation

3 Turn the adjectives into *-ly* adverbs. Check the spelling rules for each group.

1	steady	temporary	necessary	extraordinary
	....	....	....	....
2	reasonable	preferable	suitable	considerable
	....	....	....	....
3	active	close	alternative	desperate
	....	....	....	....
4	accidental	gradual	mental	potential
	....	....	....	....

4 Complete each sentence with an adverb from Exercise 3.

1 The amount of homework we get varies .... from teacher to teacher.
2 The photographs of insects in my science book are .... beautiful.
3 We could go to our usual skatepark, or .... we could try the new one that's just opened.
4 Top athletes put as much effort into being .... prepared as into being physically prepared.
5 I love maths and subjects .... related to it, like chemistry and physics.
6 I don't think your proposal is .... the best way forward – let's look at other options.
7 Josh was .... happy with his test results, but felt he could have done a bit better.
8 When my mum gave up eating sugar, she cut down .... instead of stopping suddenly.

Vocabulary

-ing and -ed adjectives

1 Choose the correct adjective to complete each sentence.

1 When my brother completed his half-marathon race, he was absolutely **exhausted** / **exhausting**.
2 The exhibition on Ancient Egypt was **fascinated** / **fascinating**.
3 A lot of **thrilled** / **thrilling** tennis matches have been played on Wimbledon Centre Court.
4 I was deeply **moved** / **moving** when my granny gave me a gold necklace.
5 I find being out in nature an incredibly **relaxed** / **relaxing** experience.
6 The news was full of **distressed** / **distressing** stories, so I watched something else.
7 I was **astonished** / **astonishing** to hear I had won the art competition.
8 When our dog went missing it was a **worried** / **worrying** time for us, but luckily, she came home by herself.

Word building

2 Make nouns from each of the words using the suffixes from the box.

-ism	-ness	-ship	-t/sion

1	apply	application	7	lazy	....
2	confuse	....	8	partner	....
3	criticise	....	9	race	....
4	dark	....	10	relation	....
5	identify	....	11	weak	....
6	journalist	....	12	willing	....

3 Make one or more adjectives from each of the words using the suffixes from the box.

-able	-ful	-ish	-less	-ous

1	adventure	adventurous
2	child	.................., ...
3	end	....
4	fool	....
5	harm	.................., ...
6	hope	.................., ...
7	mystery	....
8	predict	....
9	price	....
10	profit	....
11	skill	....
12	suspect	....

4 Complete the sentences with words from Exercises 2 and 3.

1 At the end of the basketball match there was some .... over whether we had won or lost.

2 The man's refusal to answer questions made the police ....

3 I had never completed a job .... before, so it took me ages to fill in the form.

4 The teacher accused me of ...., but it was unfair as I had worked very hard on the project.

5 It was a good film but the ending was totally .... – we all guessed what would happen.

6 Unfortunately I've always been .... at sport, even though I enjoy it.

7 When we were in Spain we visited a palace full of .... works of art.

8 After a lot of research, the biologist was able to make an accurate .... of the insect.

9 I really appreciate my teacher's .... to help me, even outside of lesson time.

10 My brother is a very .... person. He's always trying something new.

Reading and Use of English

Part 3

Need help? Go to Exam tips page 19 in the Student's Book

✓ Exam task

For questions **1–8**, read the text below. Use the word given in capitals at the end of some of the lines to form a word that fits in the gap in the same line. There is an example at the beginning (**0**).

Example: 0 SCENERY

Whale watching in Norway

Last November, I went on a whale-watching trip with my parents through the gorgeous Arctic (**0**) .... of northern Norway.	SCENE
We departed from Tromsø early in the morning. The sea was rough, so the first part of the journey was a bit (**1**) .... But I didn't mind – the views were absolutely	COMFORT
(**2**) .... We all agreed that we had never been in such stunning	BREATH
(**3**)	SURROUND
We were lucky enough to see killer whales, dolphins and humpback whales. Our boat had an electric engine, which meant we could approach the animals (**4**) .... and avoid disturbing them. The whole	SILENT
experience felt very (**5**)	PEACE
The boat itself was lovely. There was a good (**6**) .... of food and drinks	SELECT
available and the (**7**) .... on board was excellent. All in all, it was a very enjoyable trip and also an	SERVE
(**8**) .... one. I highly recommend it.	EDUCATION

3 Performance

Listening

Part 4

1 Read the exam task instructions and the exam questions carefully. Underline the important words.

Need help? Go to Exam tip page 24 in the Student's Book

✓ Exam task

🔊 **04** You will hear an interview with a teenager called Alice Fields, who runs a film club at her school. For questions **1–7**, choose the best answer (**A**, **B** or **C**).

1 Alice started her film club because
   A she wanted to share her passion with others.
   B she felt it would be helpful for her future career.
   C she was frustrated that her school didn't have one.

2 What does Alice say was difficult in the beginning?
   A getting students to join the club
   B getting permission to start the club
   C getting enough people to help run the club

3 What would Alice like teachers at her school to do?
   A become members of her club
   B interfere as little as possible in the club
   C share ideas for films to watch at the club

4 What is Alice's priority on club nights?
   A ensuring people show respect for each other
   B making sure everyone learns something
   C creating as realistic an experience as possible

5 In running the club, Alice gets a lot of pleasure from
   A mixing with people of all ages.
   B strengthening her knowledge of film.
   C witnessing the development of friendships.

6 What is Alice's attitude towards teaching students how to write reviews?
   A It's easier than it seems.
   B Being controversial is good.
   C Following a set method is a mistake.

7 What advice does Alice give about starting a club?
   A don't insist on regular attendance
   B be flexible about the timetable
   C limit the number of helpers you take on

Vocabulary

Music

1 Complete each sentence with the correct form of the word at the end of the line.

1 My parents like .... music but I prefer rap. **CLASSIC**
2 We only had six days of .... before the concert. **REHEARSE**
3 When the band's lead .... finished his solo, the audience went wild. **GUITAR**
4 The .... stands in front of the orchestra and helps everyone keep time. **CONDUCT**
5 In some popular orchestras, all the .... wear colourful historical costumes. **MUSIC**
6 The celebrations included displays of .... music and dancing. **TRADITION**
7 The .... of this piece of music was only 24 years old. **COMPOSE**
8 Most bands are much happier playing live than in a .... studio. **RECORD**

Reading and Use of English

Part 7

1 Look at the exam task and answer the questions.

1 What is the overall topic of this task?
2 What are the four people doing in these texts?
3 Skim the texts. What instrument does each person play?

Need help? Go to Exam tip page 38 in the Student's Book

You are going to read an article about four teenagers who play in orchestras. For questions **1–10**, choose from the teenagers (**A–D**). The teenagers may be chosen more than once.

Which teenager

says that it's possible to get away with making mistakes when playing in an orchestra?	1
explains why it's important to put in a lot of practice?	2
says that the key to playing in an orchestra is being able to connect with others?	3
has to force themselves to practise?	4
says that joining an orchestra didn't live up to their expectations?	5
explains what it was that inspired them to take up an instrument?	6
mentions that their standard of play has improved since joining an orchestra?	7
doubted whether the orchestra they joined would be any good?	8
is motivated in part by the pleasure they get from performing?	9
says that getting used to playing in an orchestra took time?	10

What's so great about playing in an orchestra?

Four teenagers share their experiences

A Oli I play violin and I'm currently in my school orchestra and a local community orchestra. I do it for lots of reasons. The social side is a big part of it, and so is the excitement of concert day. Being on stage and sensing the appreciation of the audience is a great feeling. It's also about developing as a musician – I have a teacher of course, but I pick loads up from my fellow players. I've really noticed the difference. Also, I've discovered that to properly feel what it's like to play in an orchestra, it's vital that you know your part thoroughly. You need to go over it again and again on your own. Only when you've done that can you begin to focus on actually making music with other people.

B Jessie I've recently joined my school orchestra. I was starting to get a bit fed up with just practising my flute on my own in my room, and I wanted that magical experience of playing with others that you hear so much about. It didn't turn out quite like that. You sit for hours on a hard chair, the person sitting next to you hasn't practised, and the conductor spends far too much time talking. I'm going to carry on doing it for a bit, though, as my teacher thinks it'll be good for me. And there is one big plus as far as I'm concerned. When you go wrong, it's not as apparent as when you're performing solo. That makes playing a lot less stressful.

C Toby When I was little, I was taken to see a professional orchestra, and after that I begged my mum to let me have trumpet lessons. I didn't get any orchestra experience until last year, though, when I finally got the chance to join one. It was a totally new way of making music for me, and I had to figure out how to adapt. What I slowly came to realise is that you have to put your individuality to one side. It's the group that matters. You have to feel that, and try to play as a whole. What's weird is that when I do this, pieces that I find very challenging to play during practice suddenly flow from my fingers. The music seems to be playing itself.

D Lucy I play in a multi-generational orchestra – one where all ages are welcome. A group of teachers, including mine, started it as a way of giving their pupils a chance to meet and play with other musicians. As well as being a mix of ages, we're also a mix of abilities, and in the beginning I wasn't sure it was going to work. In the end it did, and our evolution from a random bunch of strangers into an actual orchestra that can make wonderful sounds has been so rewarding. What's tough for me is learning my part at home before proper rehearsals begin. I play what's called second violin, so I don't play the melody. My part on its own doesn't sound much like music, and it takes a lot of discipline on my part to make myself learn it.

Vocabulary

Film and theatre

1 Match the words from the box with their meanings.

> cast   dialogue   double act   entertaining
> genre   plot   release   script   series
> soundtrack   special effects   themes

1   ideas running through a film/book ....
2   funny and enjoyable ....
3   two entertainers who perform together ....
4   the written text of a film or play ....
5   the actors in a film or show ....
6   a category of book, film, etc. ....
7   a set of stories that are related ....
8   the music of a film or show ....
9   the story of a book, film, etc. ....
10   conversation between characters ....
11   to make a film, etc. available ....
12   techniques used to create images ....

2 Use the words from Exercise 1 to complete the blog post below. Make changes to the words if necessary.

Grammar

Linking words and phrases

1 Match the two halves of the sentences.

1   Our new flat is bigger than our last one
2   Despite the danger,
3   We had a good time on holiday
4   The film was well acted and the story was interesting –
5   The children enjoyed the trip to the theme park
6   I asked my mum if I could go to the party
7   In spite of the fact that Gemma was a beginner,
8   I bought the trainers

a   however, at three hours, it was far too long.
b   although I knew she'd probably say no.
c   the photographer made his way to the top of the cliff.
d   even though I couldn't really afford them.
e   she won the chess match.
f   but it's much noisier.
g   in spite of the awful weather.
h   despite the long queues for the rides.

Treeway High School
Student blog
Today's contributor: Ali Bell
A classic film from the 1990s you might enjoy!

I'm going to write about a film my parents introduced me to – it's called *Men in Black,* and it was **(1)** .... back in 1997. What makes it so great is the way it mixes different movie **(2)** .... – it's a comedy, a science-fiction movie, and an action movie all at once. The **(3)** .... are secrecy, power and friendship.

The film is based on a little-known Marvel comic **(4)** .... of the same name, by a writer called Lowell Cunningham. The central idea is that aliens have been living on Earth for decades and are being monitored by government agents, who must keep their existence a secret. The **(5)** .... is excellent, especially the stars. Will Smith plays a fresh-faced young agent, taken

on to work with the much more experienced Agent K, played by Tommy Lee Jones. The pair make a hilarious **(6)** .... Jones is serious, business-like and unsmiling, while Will Smith bounces around, full of energy and silliness. The contrast between the two is highly **(7)** ....

It's true that the **(8)** .... is rather unbelievable and sometimes I felt that the **(9)** .... had been written mainly to present lots of action scenes. However, the **(10)** .... between the main characters is witty throughout and the **(11)** .... are surprisingly good. The aliens come in all shapes and sizes and are cleverly imagined. I loved all the inventive gadgets too.

The music is a big highlight. The **(12)** .... was made into an album, and the theme song, performed by Will Smith himself, was his first solo single. It won him a Grammy Award.

The passive

2 Rewrite the sentences in the passive, using the word given.

1 Next year, the school will buy new chairs for the main hall.
BE
New chairs .... for the school hall next year.

2 Are they opening a new theatre in our town?
OPENED
Is a new theatre .... in our town?

3 No one told me that auditions for the school play were happening today!
BEEN
I should .... that auditions for the school play were happening today!

4 TV executives are going to cancel my favourite comedy show next year!
TO
My favourite comedy show is .... next year!

5 The man fell while someone was helping him across the road.
BEING
The man .... across the road when he fell.

6 Nowadays, the law protects many types of birds of prey.
BY
Nowadays, many types of birds of prey .... the law.

have something done

3 Rewrite the sentences below using *have* + noun + past participle.

1 I was surprised when someone dyed my friend's hair pink.
I was surprised when my friend .... pink.

2 My parents asked someone to build a summer house at the bottom of the garden.
My parents .... at the bottom of the garden.

3 Mum wants someone to take photos of us so she can put them on the walls.
Mum wants .... of us so she can put them on the walls.

4 Someone is fixing my bike so I can cycle to school again.
I'm .... so I can cycle to school again.

Reading and Use of English

Part 4

Need help? Go to Exam tip page 29 in the Student's Book

✓ Exam task

For questions **1–6**, complete the second sentence so that it has a similar meaning to the first sentence, using the word given. **Do not change the word given**. You must use between **two** and **five** words, including the word given. Here is an example (**0**).

Example:

0 The train's expensive so I'd prefer to take the bus.
RATHER
The train's expensive so I
.... WOULD RATHER .... take the bus.

1 Doctors say you should go for an eye test every two years.
EYES
Doctors say you should
.... tested every two years.

2 The teacher didn't know about the problems I'd had completing the homework.
UNAWARE
The teacher .... the problems I'd had completing the homework.

3 Yesterday I heard from an old friend that I last saw two years ago!
SEEN
Yesterday I heard from an old friend that I
.... two years!

4 I probably won't get my project finished tonight.
UNLIKELY
I .... my project tonight.

5 There are fewer fish in the sea today than there were a decade ago.
AS
There .... fish in the sea today as there were a decade ago.

6 Sue's performance in the concert was shockingly bad.
AT
I was .... badly Sue performed in the concert.

Reading and Use of English

Part 5

1 Look at the exam task. Read the text once quickly and answer the questions.

1 Who does Katie Zelem play football for now?
2 Who did she use to play football for?
3 What honour was Katie Zelem awarded?

Need help? Go to Exam tip page 30 in the Student's Book

✓ Exam task

You are going to read an article about a professional football player. For questions **1–4**, choose the answer (**A**, **B**, **C** or **D**) which you think fits best according to the text.

1 How did Katie feel when she signed her contract with Juventus?
   A confused about what to take with her
   B shocked that she had to leave home so early
   C impatient to tell her family and friends
   D unwilling to change the agreed schedule

2 What effect did meeting Katie Rood have on Zelem?
   A It helped her settle in to her new surroundings.
   B It focused her mind on her reasons for being in Turin.
   C It taught her not to make instant judgements on others.
   D It showed her she was not the only one who was struggling.

3 The writer uses the phrase 'did not let this go to her head' in line 36 to let the reader know that Zelem isn't
   A bitter.
   B uneasy.
   C arrogant.
   D embarrassed.

4 What point is the writer making about Alan Zelem in the final paragraph?
   A He misses playing football with his family a great deal.
   B His football career caused him a lot of physical damage.
   C Without his help his daughter wouldn't have succeeded.
   D His daughter is a much stronger player than him these days.

Manchester United captain, Katie Zelem

Interviewed by Louise Taylor

Katie Zelem has very clear memories of the moment she signed the contract that finalised her move from Liverpool Football Club to Juventus, a top Italian club based in Turin. 'I was immediately told: "We've booked you on a flight tomorrow",' she recalls. 'I said it was impossible. I needed time to pack, I had to buy new clothes and I hadn't had a chance to say goodbye to my family and my friends. In the end I pushed it back by a few days, but I still didn't manage to empty the house where I lived in Liverpool.'

When Zelem landed in northern Italy back in August 2017, the culture shock was powerful. 'The full extent of my Italian ran to "ciao", so nothing was straightforward. For the first week I thought: "Wow, what have I done?" ' But a city-centre flat-share with a teammate, the New Zealand international Katie Rood, transformed the experience. 'Katie and I still get on really well,' says Zelem. 'But it's the most unlikely friendship – no one can believe we like each other. The thing is, we were thrown together and had to make it work. Living abroad does that to you. It made me independent – and left me with a lot of respect for all the overseas players coping so well in England.'

The following year, Zelem returned to England for a new challenge. Manager Casey Stoney was creating a professional Manchester United women's team from scratch, and Zelem was appointed captain. At the end of the team's first season, they were promoted to the Women's Super League and Zelem was voted the club's first female 'player of the year'. She subsequently appeared alongside two leading male players on a huge painting on a wall in the city's Northern Quarter. Unsurprisingly, given how down-to-earth she is, Zelem
36 did not let this go to her head. 'I haven't gone past there for a long time and I think it's been painted over now,' she says.

Of course, her family are immensely proud of her. She is the daughter of Alan Zelem, a former professional goalkeeper, and niece of Peter Zelem, a former defender. Alan devoted countless hours to coaching the young Katie in their back garden, but with a hip replacement to protect and the need to stay agile for his work as a window cleaner, he no longer dares challenge her to a kickabout.

Listening

1 Look at the exam task. Read the instructions and the ten sentences. Answer the questions.

1 Will Louise talk about the history of paddle boarding? Which sentences suggest this?

2 Will Louise compare paddle boarding with another sport? Which sentence suggests this?

3 Which sentence will you complete with a number?

4 Which sentences will you complete with a verb, an adjective, a noun or noun phrase?

Need help? Go to Exam tip page 32 in the Student's Book

✓ Exam task

🔊 **05** You will hear a teenager called Louise Porter giving a class presentation about a water sport called paddle boarding. For questions **1–10**, complete the sentences with a word or short phrase.

Paddle boarding

1 Louise was surprised to learn that .... was one of the reasons ancient cultures used boards.

2 Louise says that the number of people trying paddle boarding began to increase dramatically .... years ago.

3 Louise uses the word .... to describe the type of exercise you get when you paddle board.

4 Louise says that learning to paddle board is easier than learning to ....

5 Louise had a scary encounter with a .... while paddle boarding recently.

6 Louise feels that .... aren't as much of a problem on a paddle board as they are on a kayak.

7 Louise is going to try paddle boarding combined with .... in the near future.

8 Louise disapproves of the idea of attaching a .... to a paddle board.

9 One advantage of the type of paddle board Louise uses is that it can be put into a ....

10 Louise does not go paddle boarding in .... conditions.

Vocabulary

Health care

1 Complete the email with the words from the box.

| aching | bruise | heal | injury | recovery |
| strained | surgery | swollen | therapy | X-ray |

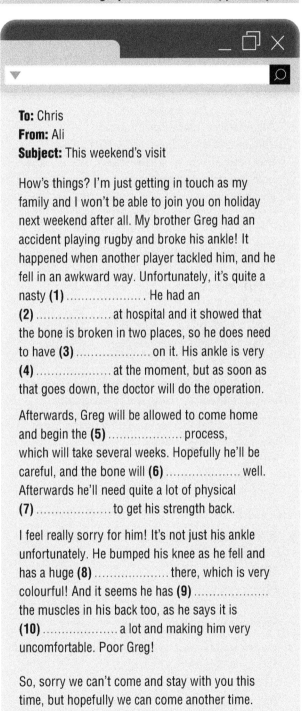

To: Chris
From: Ali
Subject: This weekend's visit

How's things? I'm just getting in touch as my family and I won't be able to join you on holiday next weekend after all. My brother Greg had an accident playing rugby and broke his ankle! It happened when another player tackled him, and he fell in an awkward way. Unfortunately, it's quite a nasty **(1)** .... He had an **(2)** .... at hospital and it showed that the bone is broken in two places, so he does need to have **(3)** .... on it. His ankle is very **(4)** .... at the moment, but as soon as that goes down, the doctor will do the operation.

Afterwards, Greg will be allowed to come home and begin the **(5)** .... process, which will take several weeks. Hopefully he'll be careful, and the bone will **(6)** .... well. Afterwards he'll need quite a lot of physical **(7)** .... to get his strength back.

I feel really sorry for him! It's not just his ankle unfortunately. He bumped his knee as he fell and has a huge **(8)** .... there, which is very colourful! And it seems he has **(9)** .... the muscles in his back too, as he says it is **(10)** .... a lot and making him very uncomfortable. Poor Greg!

So, sorry we can't come and stay with you this time, but hopefully we can come another time.

Word building

2 Complete each sentence with the correct form of the word at the end of the line.

1 I had a bad .... to some seafood so we had to leave the restaurant. **REACT**

2 We've tried to make sure there are no .... plants in our garden. **POISON**

3 Recent advances in .... technology have been incredible. **MEDICINE**

4 When I applied the cream, I had a brief burning .... on my skin. **SENSE**

5 The doctor gave the patient a thorough .... **EXAM**

6 The hike was fun but far more .... demanding than I expected. **PHYSICAL**

7 It's important to work towards ending .... in the world. **SUFFER**

8 It's well known that some illnesses have a .... cause. **PSYCHOLOGY**

Grammar
Modal verbs

1 Complete the second sentence so it has a similar meaning to the first, using the word given.

1 I'm sure our neighbour has a new puppy because I can hear it crying at night.
   HAVE
   Our new neighbour
   .... a new puppy because I can hear it crying at night.

2 When I was little, I could speak German but I can't any more!
   ABLE
   When I was little, I
   .... speak German but I can't any more!

3 It was a mistake not to check the weather forecast before we left for the beach.
   SHOULD
   We .... the weather forecast before we left for the beach.

4 It's possible that Dad left this money on the table for me.
   MIGHT
   Dad .... this money on the table for me.

5 It hasn't been possible for us to play tennis as the courts are frozen.
   ABLE
   We .... to play tennis as the courts are frozen.

6 It's important that I take my science project to school tomorrow.
   REMEMBER
   I .... take my science project to school tomorrow.

7 It's not necessary to have a large income to have a happy life.
   NEED
   You .... to have a large income to have a happy life.

8 I'm sure it wasn't Sam you saw because he's away on holiday.
   BEEN
   It .... Sam you saw because he's away on holiday.

2 Complete the sentences using the verbs in brackets in the correct form. You may need to change the tense or make one of the verbs negative.

1 Don't get too excited – we .... (may / see) any wildlife on the safari, but hopefully we will.

2 You .... (should / book) those tickets before they all sold out.

3 I .... (must / forget) to reply to my friend's message!

4 It's such a shame we .... (can / spend) the summer together.

5 I'll ask Dad but I'm afraid he .... (might / let) me come with you to the lake.

6 The only thing I dislike about playing the violin is that I .... (have / practise) scales every day.

7 Last night's maths homework .... (should / be) easy for me, but I got all the answers wrong!

8 You .... (need / give) me the money today – tomorrow's fine.

9 Somebody .... (must / forget) to tell Jim about the room change for band practice.

10 Don't worry, you .... (have / go) to the party if you don't want to.

Prepositions: *at, in, on*

3 Choose the correct preposition to complete each sentence.

1 Please don't talk! I really need to concentrate **on / at** this science video.
2 My sister is waiting for us **in / at** the bus stop.
3 Try not to let your interest **in / on** video games interfere with your schoolwork.
4 Toby is amazing – he's fluent **in / at** six languages!
5 The delivery driver is **on / at** the back door.
6 **On / In** the whole, it was a really good trip.

Reading and Use of English

Part 2

1 Correct each sentence using a word in bold from another sentence.

1 My school has produced several famous people, **apart** we're all very proud of.
2 Everyone worked hard, and **instead** a result, the exhibition was a huge success.
3 We stayed in a hotel this year **which** of camping, like we usually do.
4 Doing team sports **but** as hockey is said to improve your critical-thinking skills.
5 What sets Harvey **mine** from the rest of us is how good he is at sport.
6 School trips are important not only academically, **up** for social reasons too.
7 Josh is a good friend of **as** – I've known him since I was ten.
8 The report stated that **such** to 20% of teenagers are addicted to social media.

Need help? Go to Exam tip page 34 in the Student's Book

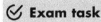 **Exam task**

For questions **1–8**, read the text below and think of the word which best fits each gap. Use only one word in each gap. There is an example at the beginning (**0**).

Example: 0 HOW

We all know **(0)** .... important it is to be active, and most of us are full of good intentions. However, actually getting **(1)** .... to doing it is more of a challenge. Luckily though, **(2)** .... are ways to build exercise into your routine that don't involve making a huge effort.

Firstly, for those of you **(3)** .... live within walking distance of your school, making the journey on foot is a great way to start your day. Then, once you're at school, make the **(4)** .... of your breaks. Head outside for a walk or play sport with friends.

Later, you might find yourself sitting to do homework or watch TV. In that case, make sure you stand up at **(5)** .... once an hour.

Finally, **(6)** .... it might not sound like lots of fun, doing household chores is great exercise. It doesn't **(7)** .... whether it's vacuuming or cutting the grass, you'll be raising your heart rate and working muscles **(8)** .... even realising it.

Listening

Part 2

1 Read the exam task instructions and answer the questions.

1 Would you like to do a course like this? Do you think it would be useful?

2 How many possible answers can you think of for gap 8?

Need help? Go to Exam tips page 40 in the Student's Book

✓ Exam task

◁)) **06** You will hear a man called Paul Mathers talking about a summer technology camp for teenagers. For questions **1–10**, complete the sentences with a word or short phrase.

Residential technology camp

Paul says that students on the residential course will share a **(1)** .... with a few other people.

It is possible to book what is known as a **(2)** .... if you want to stay for a few more days.

Students who do not sleep at the college should arrive by **(3)** .... a.m.

An evening activity called **(4)** .... is being introduced for the first time.

Paul says that recent developments in technology related to **(5)** .... mean it's a topic that must be included in the course.

Paul says that the **(6)** .... given to students is a great way to begin the day.

Paul uses the word **(7)** .... to describe the atmosphere of the morning lecture.

Paul gives the example of creating a **(8)** .... as something practical that students might be asked to do.

Paul says that some tutors at the camp have gone on to get jobs as **(9)** ....

Parents of students on the camp will be contacted daily by **(10)** .... to let them know how the course is going.

Reading and Use of English

Part 7

1 Look at the study tips below. Tick (✓) the ones you regularly do. How effective do you think they are?

1 study in short sessions
2 make notes and then rewrite them
3 schedule time to study
4 use coloured pens and highlighters
5 focus on understanding the meaning of what you are learning
6 get lots of sleep and study when you are refreshed
7 get friends and family to test you
8 have one place where you always study

2 Read the article once and check which study tips are mentioned. Which ones does the psychologist say are not effective? Do you agree?

Need help? Go to Exam tip page 38 in the Student's Book

You are going to read a magazine article about study habits. For questions **1–10**, choose from the sections **A–D**. The sections may be chosen more than once.

In which section does the writer mention

the importance of connecting facts together as you study?	**1**
a decision to do things differently?	**2**
the benefits of creating and sticking to a plan?	**3**
a technique that should be followed closely?	**4**
a failure to pass crucial information on?	**5**
a step in a strategy that should not be missed out?	**6**
the fact that some techniques can be applied universally?	**7**
something that young people should bear in mind more than they do?	**8**
a popular but ineffective technique?	**9**
a little-known finding that is of particular interest?	**10**

What's the best way to study?

Psychologist Anna Peterson takes a look at the science behind this very important question.

A When I was a teenager, I was very keen on stationery. I had a huge collection of coloured highlighters and I would mark up bits of text in my books. The idea was that when I went back over the material, the colours would tell me different things. But once the time came, I could never remember what they were supposed to mean. The other thing I did was something students everywhere still do – I took loads of notes, and then rewrote the notes in different words later on. It improved my handwriting, but not much else. By the time I got to college, I felt I was really starting to struggle. It became apparent that I was in serious need of a study skills upgrade, so I started looking into the science around the subject.

B I discovered that for over 100 years, psychologists have been carrying out research into what study skills work best. However, for some reason this is rarely communicated to students. Instead, they are expected to just get on with it – it's a bit like telling someone who can't swim to 'just swim'. This is a great disservice in my opinion. As it turns out, there are a number of proven strategies that work for almost every subject. One of the most important is to fully understand what it is you are learning. It's very hard to remember information that's just a list of unrelated details. You should always take class material and ask a lot of how and why questions about it. Having the extra information will help you link bits of information from elsewhere, and create a larger network of knowledge in your brain.

C One of the best ways to really get information into your head is to quiz yourself on it, or get someone else to quiz you. This could be a parent or a friend – but what's crucial is that it's done in precisely the way a teacher might do it. It's no good unless you are asked to really dig deep and think hard. What's fascinating, and what most people do not realise, is that the research shows that spending ages thinking about the answer is no more effective than taking just a couple of seconds to do so. And coming up with the answer is not essential either – the strategy is just as effective if you look up the answer, or are told it by someone else. But what you should never do is skip this part – it seems to be where the learning occurs.

D Don't worry about making mistakes – they are key to learning. Most students are actually aware of this now, but sadly that doesn't stop them being angry with themselves when they get things wrong. It's very important to be kind to yourself, and avoid stressing yourself out if things don't go right. One thing that will help hugely is putting together a schedule, and then making sure you follow it. It means you will need a lot less willpower on a daily basis. Remember, it's been shown that several short sessions are far more effective than a few longer ones, even if the total number of hours spent studying is identical. Set a timer for 25 minutes, then take a five- or ten-minute break. Check your phone, walk around a bit, have a drink of water. Then set the timer again.

Vocabulary

Phrasal verbs *get* and *go*

1 Complete each gap with the correct form of *get* or *go*, so that the phrasal verb matches the meaning given in brackets at the end of the sentence.

1 I .... through my notes before the test to make sure I understood them properly. (examine)
2 We have to hide the chocolate in our house so my little brother can't .... at it. (reach or touch)
3 It took me ages to .... over my last cold; I'm not sure why. (recover from)
4 I used to like mint-flavoured ice cream, but recently I've .... off it. (stopped liking)
5 I didn't want to do the washing up but Mum wouldn't let me .... out of it. (avoid something)
6 I finally .... round to cleaning my room last night and it looks great. (found time)
7 Dad was late for dinner so he told us to .... ahead without him. (start)
8 I couldn't really understand the point the teacher was making so I asked her to .... over it again. (explain in a detailed way)

2 Choose the correct preposition to complete each sentence.

1 Sally went **up** / **over** / **on** talking even though we asked her to be quiet.
2 When my friend was going **around** / **along** / **through** a tough time with her parents, I supported her as well as I could.
3 The teacher only asked for a two-page essay, but I got carried **along** / **over** / **away** and ended up doing ten!
4 I'm not sure about trying out for the basketball team but my friend says I should go **at** / **for** / **with** it.
5 Some teachers are really good at getting information **across** / **on** / **up** in an interesting way.
6 When the fireworks went **in** / **off** / **on** they made an incredibly loud noise.
7 The film was three hours long but the time went **by** / **over** / **along** very quickly.

Grammar

wish, if only and regrets

1 Complete the paragraph by choosing the correct form of each verb.

What I did was so stupid! I **(1) shouldn't** / **couldn't** have invited all my friends over to my house when my parents went away for the weekend. I really regret **(2) doing** / **to do** it! If only I **(3) have been** / **had been** more sensible! Inviting Jake was my biggest mistake. I wish he **(4) hadn't broken** / **didn't break** my mother's favourite vase! But I'm fed up of being told off now. I wish my parents **(5) hadn't been** / **weren't** still so cross about it. If only they **(6) knew** / **had known** how sorry I am!

2 Complete the sentences with the correct form of the verb in brackets.

1 I wish I .... (get) to the top of the mountain, but the weather was against me.
2 If only I .... (remember) her name, she wouldn't have been so upset.
3 I'd rather we .... (meet) in town, if you don't mind?
4 My brother wishes he .... (be) as tall as me.
5 I'd rather you .... (not play) your music so loudly.
6 If only my parents .... (let) me get a dog!
7 I wish I .... (not trip up) the defender in the penalty box!
8 I'd rather we .... (work) on the project separately if that's OK?
9 I wish my dad .... (not have to) travel so much with his job.
10 It was a good party but I wished I .... (wear) something smarter.

Conditionals

3 Complete the second sentence so it has a similar meaning to the first sentence, using the word given.

1 The only way to get good results is to study hard.
    IF
    You won't get good results .... study hard.
2 You'll get there on time if you succeed in catching the 4.20 bus.
    MANAGE
    You'll get there on time as .... catch the 4.20 bus.
3 The teacher said she'd let us go home early provided we left the classroom tidy.
    ONLY
    The teacher said we .... if we left the classroom clean and tidy.

4 Amy couldn't find her bike so she had to walk to school.

HAVE

If Amy had been able to find her bike, she

.... to walk to school.

5 I could help if I knew the answer!

BECAUSE

I .... I don't know the answer!

6 You might get bored on the journey, so take a good book with you.

CASE

Take a good book on the journey with you .... get bored.

7 You can't pass the test if you don't study!

IMPOSSIBLE

Passing the test will

.... you study!

8 I regret telling Sophia my secret.

WISH

I .... Sophia my secret.

Reading and Use of English

Part 1

Need help? Go to Exam tip page 42 in the Student's Book

✓ Exam task

For questions **1–8**, read the text opposite and decide which answer (**A**, **B**, **C** or **D**) best fits each gap. There is an example at the beginning (**0**).

Example: 0

A acts   B represents   C proceeds   D runs

1	**A** basis	**B** roots	**C** sources	**D** background
2	**A** increased	**B** stretched	**C** grown	**D** spread
3	**A** give	**B** express	**C** encourage	**D** raise
4	**A** boost	**B** multiply	**C** extend	**D** motivate
5	**A** think	**B** count	**C** see	**D** understand
6	**A** ready	**B** possible	**C** arranged	**D** open
7	**A** happen	**B** present	**C** arrive	**D** result
8	**A** try	**B** struggle	**C** effort	**D** duty

The value of having a mentor

A mentor is an individual who **(0)** ....A........ as an advisor or coach for someone less experienced and knowledgeable than them. It's a concept that has its **(1)** .... in the business world, but in recent years it has **(2)** .... more widely into society. There's now a lot of evidence that it can be very helpful for teenagers, too. Research shows that having a non-parent mentor can **(3)** .... new ways of thinking, **(4)** .... confidence, and help teenagers interpret and manage life's challenges. It seems that mentoring relationships are most successful when mentors don't **(5)** .... themselves as instructors, advisors or role models, but as listeners and supporters.

Formal mentoring programmes do exist, but these are not usually **(6)** .... to everyone. It is possible for informal mentoring relationships to arise naturally, perhaps with a teacher, sports coach or neighbour, but this does not **(7)** .... for most teens. Therefore, teenagers should make a conscious **(8)** .... to find themselves a mentor, just as many young professionals have learnt to do.

Our planet

Listening

Part 4

1 Read the exam task and questions quickly. What do you think is meant by a 'zero-waste' life?

2 Most Listening Part 4 items are about the speaker's attitude and opinion, but sometimes there is a factual question. Which of the questions 1–7 below is about a fact?

Need help? Go to Exam tips page 47 in the Student's Book

☑ Exam task

🔊 07   You will hear an interview with a young blogger called Emma, who's talking about living a 'zero-waste' life. For questions **1–7**, choose the best answer (**A**, **B** or **C**).

1 What does Emma say about famous zero-waste bloggers?
   A They are the reason she got interested in the topic.
   B She'd like to be as well known as they are.
   C There's no way she can achieve what they do.

2 How does Emma feel about the term zero-waste?
   A It's a bit misleading.
   B It's popular with journalists.
   C People use it who have no right to.

3 Emma accepts that her attitude towards waste
   A is something she will always need to work on.
   B causes problems between her and her family.
   C may have been influenced by her upbringing.

4 Why did Emma carry out a survey in her neighbourhood?
   A It was a compulsory piece of schoolwork.
   B Her teacher needed help completing a project.
   C She wanted to prove something to those living near her.

5 How does Emma feel about stopping using drinking straws?
   A It was a silly thing to do.
   B It was an important first step.
   C It was a life-changing decision.

6 Emma says people just starting out with zero-waste should avoid
   A choosing products that are unlikely to last long.
   B rushing to get rid of items they already own.
   C being taken advantage of by certain companies.

7 What does Emma say about mistakes?
   A They are to be expected.
   B She makes rather a lot of them.
   C She is getting better at accepting them.

Vocabulary

The environment

1 Choose the correct heading for each paragraph. Then complete the gapped words.

   1 Electric cars and buses
   2 Environmental monitoring
   3 Lab-grown food
   4 Solar glass panels
   5 Trainers made from waste

How technology is helping save the environment

A ....

Scientists have been working on a **(1)** t _ _ _ s p _ _ _ _ t material that can produce energy. They hope to be able to use it in place of normal windows, as this would be an easy way to **(2)** g _ _ _ r _ _ _ electricity if it was installed in enough homes.

B ....

People love to eat meat but farm animals are responsible for around 15 percent of greenhouse **(3)** g _ s _ _. Synthetic meat could be the answer, if it can be made appealing enough to consumers.

C ....

A sustainable fashion brand from Helsinki is using the grounds left over from making coffee, together with **(4)** r _ _ _ _ _ _ d plastic bottles, to create high-performance, waterproof footwear.

D ....

Laws are now in place all over the world to protect wildlife and maintain air **(5)** q _ _ _ _ _ _. However, there will always be those who continue to **(6)** p _ l _ _ _ _ rivers and farmland, or kill wildlife. Technology such as drones and satellites can be used to record this activity and prevent criminal behaviour.

E ....

As long as these are powered from **(7)** r _ n _ w _ b _ _ sources such as wind and solar, they are far less **(8)** h _ _ _ f _ _ to the environment than traditional vehicles. There are environmental problems associated with the production of batteries, but it is hoped these can be solved.

Grammar

too and enough

1 Correct these common exam candidate mistakes.

1 The book wasn't enough interesting so I stopped reading it.
2 It's a long way and we are so tired to walk.
3 I wanted to look at the view, but the window was to dirty.
4 The exam was hard because time wasn't enough to finish it.
5 If we go for a swim today we'll be so cold to enjoy it.
6 This cookbook is good because the instructions aren't hard enough.

so and such

2 Choose *so* or *such* in these sentences written by exam candidates.

1 Jane should do well at tennis because she's **so / such** good at squash and badminton.
2 The teachers on the course were **so / such** friendly people.
3 I don't know how you manage to keep your hair looking **so / such** great.
4 The children had **so / such** a good time at the ice show.
5 My granny has **so / such** good memories of her childhood.
6 There were **so / such** many choices on the menu, we couldn't choose.

Reading and Use of English

Part 2

Need help? Go to Exam tip page 53 in the Student's Book

✓ Exam task

For questions **1–8**, read the text below and think of the word which best fits each gap. Use only **one** word in each gap. There is an example at the beginning (**0**).

Example: 0 OF

Stick insects

Stick insects are astonishing creatures, and come in a huge range **(0)** .... colours, shapes and sizes. **(1)** .... their name suggests, many look like sticks or branches, although **(2)** .... are some that look like leaves. Some species are **(3)** .... amazingly good at the art of disguise that it is almost impossible to see them **(4)** .... you know exactly where to look. They remain completely still during the day, **(5)** .... makes spotting them even more of a challenge. When surprised, stick insects will either move gently from side to side as **(6)** .... they have been caught in the breeze, or they will drop to the ground, where they lie very still, just like a fallen stick.

The eggs of many stick-insect species look exactly like seeds. Ants carry these into their nests, believing them to be food, and protect them **(7)** .... predators. When they hatch, the babies look and behave like ants **(8)** .... the time is right for them to escape the nest and climb into a tree.

Reading and Use of English

1 Read the exam task instructions and look at the picture. What do you think the text will be about? Read the text quickly to check your ideas.

Need help? Go to Exam tip page 50 in the Student's Book

✓ Exam task

You are going to read a newspaper article about an Ecuadorian environmentalist. Six sentences have been removed from the article. Choose from the sentences **A–G** the one which fits each gap (**1–6**). There is one extra sentence which you do not need to use.

Omar Tello, a hero of the environment

When he was a little boy in Ecuador, Omar Tello remembers being surrounded by nature. However, as the years went by, more and more of his beloved rainforest was cut down to make way for farmland. Gradually the plants, insects, birds and wild animals that were such an important part of his life disappeared.

Omar grew up, trained as an accountant and began working in a bank, but his passion for the rainforest never left him. He became obsessed with finding a patch of land that had previously been rainforest and restoring it. **(1)** .... He did not disagree with them. However, he felt unable to stand by and watch the destruction continue without doing something about it.

Eventually, in 1980, when he was 23 years old, he found and purchased a piece of land outside the town of Puyo. The piece of land was small, just seven hectares. **(2)** .... It was Omar and his wife's dream to turn it back into jungle, although at the time neither of them imagined how hard it would be to do this.

In the beginning, Omar would go to work at the bank during the day, and in the evenings and at weekends he would work on the land. **(3)** .... Because of this, he had no choice but to leave his job and concentrate full time on the forest.

Omar and his wife Lupe began by planting trees, but these failed to grow, as the soil was too poor to support them. **(4)** .... To do this, they dug organic materials such as sawdust and chicken manure into the ground, and gradually things started to grow again. At this point, Omar travelled around the Amazon to find the seeds he needed to regrow his forest.

The effect was astonishing. Not only did the trees Omar planted start growing, but native plants and animals began to return on their own. **(5)** .... The area now hosts thousands of species, some of which are incredibly rare. Omar makes a point of recording them all, and this information is of great interest to scientists.

Omar's forest is now called Jardín Botanico Las Orquídeas, and is open to the public. **(6)** .... Omar himself is considered a leader in the field, and he now spends most of his time collaborating with educational institutions, community centres and local farmers in order to show how his successes can be repeated. Unless this can be done, the loss of forest areas will continue to outweigh the gains.

A Clearly, steps would need to be taken to improve and enrich it.
B The result was that he had little to no free time and soon he was suffering the effects of stress.
C More importantly, it is recognised by many experts as an example of how an ecosystem can be restored.
D However, very few can take on the responsibility of doing so the way Omar has.
E It had been cleared of vegetation and planted with grass so it could support farm animals such as horses and cattle.
F Each one that appeared helped renew the health of the forest.
G Everyone he told about this plan, including most members of his family, thought it was crazy.

Grammar

Countable and uncountable nouns

1 Choose a noun from the box to complete each sentence. Make the noun plural if necessary.

> argument   breakthrough   evidence
> experience   impression
> lifestyle   misunderstanding
> pressure   research   rubbish

1 People's .... will have to change if we want to beat climate change.
2 My mum says she's been under quite a lot of .... at work recently.
3 I'm not sure I've got enough work .... to get a job in a shop, unfortunately.
4 'I think there's been a ....,' said the teacher. 'I wanted your homework today, not on Monday.'
5 First .... are really important when you meet new people.
6 Everyone should try to reduce the amount of .... they throw in the bin.
7 I've listened to all the .... on both sides of the recycling debate, and I still think it's a good idea.
8 I heard a podcast about some fascinating .... into bacteria last night.
9 I'm not sure there's much .... to support your ideas, I'm afraid.
10 There have been so many scientific .... recently, it's hard to keep up!

Articles

2 Correct the sentences by adding *a/an* or *the* where needed.

1 I watched most amazing documentary about Namibia at weekend.
2 My mum used to be actor and she still loves going to theatre as often as she can.
3 My brother's in hospital because he broke his leg playing in football match.
4 Bengal tiger is native to Indian subcontinent and is threatened with extinction.
5 My family and I have just had wonderful summer holiday in Alps.
6 Scientists have been trying to warn governments for many years about dangers of global warming.
7 Why don't you come round to my house after dinner tonight, and we can choose film to watch?
8 I'd love to go to concert with you in summer. I love listening to live music.

Listening

Part 3

1 Read the exam task instructions, and the options A–H. Tick (✓) the ones that match your opinions about going shopping with friends.

Need help? Go to Exam tip page 60 in the Student's Book

✓ Exam task

🔊 **08** You will hear five short extracts in which teenagers are talking about going shopping. For questions **1–5**, choose from the list (**A–H**) what each speaker says about going shopping with friends. Use the letters only once. There are three extra letters which you do not need to use.

A I find it inspiring.

B It sometimes puts me off.

C I only do it if I'm shopping for something straightforward.

D I only do it with certain people.

E It makes it harder for me to buy things.

F It helps make my friendships stronger.

G It's something I'm planning to try soon.

H It helps keep me focused.

Speaker 1	**1**
Speaker 2	**2**
Speaker 3	**3**
Speaker 4	**4**
Speaker 5	**5**

Grammar

Verbs and expressions + *to* + infinitive or *-ing* form

1 Choose a verb from the box to complete each sentence. Decide if you need to use the infinitive with *to* or the *-ing* verb form.

ask	be	change	discuss	finish	forget
give	live	pay	provide	speak	win

1 Jake refused .... out of his dirty T-shirt before dinner, even though his mum asked him to.

2 I can't imagine .... in the same house my whole life.

3 I'm not sure my team deserved .... but I'm glad they did.

4 My little brother loves pretending .... a dinosaur.

5 We try to avoid .... politics in my house, as my dad can be quite boring on the subject.

6 I considered .... for a guitar for my birthday, but decided against it.

7 I managed .... to the teacher about my homework at the end of the class.

8 I forgot my money, so I arranged .... for the school trip the next day.

9 I'm aiming .... my project tomorrow, but I'm not sure I will be able to.

10 The government suggested .... all students with a free laptop.

11 If I don't make a list, I tend .... what I need to do.

12 I decided .... a lot of my old clothes away to a charity shop.

Reported speech

2a A journalist is interviewing a young person called Callum who makes and sells cookies. Rewrite the journalist's questions in reported speech. Begin: *The journalist asked Callum …*

1 How big is your business now?
2 Will you carry on doing this when you are an adult?
3 Is there anything you regret about starting a business?
4 What advice do you have for other young entrepreneurs?

2b Match the answers below with the questions from Exercise 2a.

A I can't spend much time with my friends – that's the only thing.
B You must work hard, and don't let other people tell you that you can't succeed.
C I'll probably be bored of it by then, I think!
D I have four full-time employees, and I'll probably need to hire more soon. It's growing fast!

2c Complete the information about Callum.

1 Callum said that his business .... growing fast and that he .... probably need to hire more staff soon.
2 Callum said that he probably .... continue with the business after he grew up.
3 Callum said the only thing he regretted about running a business was that he .... spend as much time with friends as he'd like.
4 Callum said that other young entrepreneurs should work hard and not .... other people tell them they .... succeed.

3 For each sentence, choose the reporting verb that best describes what the person is doing. Then use the verb to rewrite the sentence in reported speech.

1 My sister said, 'Please, please, please come to the party with me!'
   beg / order / claim
2 'It's very important that you finish this work by Tuesday,' said the teacher.
   question / stress / propose
3 'This skateboard is the best you can get within your budget, I promise,' said the salesman.
   check / order / assure
4 'Getting Mum flowers for her birthday is an awful idea,' said my brother.
   reject / emphasise / boast
5 'I think it was a great decision of mine to buy this coat, even if you disagree!' said Dad.
   decline / stress / defend

6 'I promise you I'll be there by eight!' said Mary.
   recommend / swear / propose
7 'I'm going on a 60-kilometre solo bike ride tomorrow,' said my sister.
   declare / reject / dismiss
8 'Have you remembered your dental appointment?' asked Mum.
   question / decline / check

Reading and Use of English

Part 4

Need help? Go to Exam tip page 59 in the Student's Book

☑ Exam task

For questions **1–6**, complete the second sentence so that it has a similar meaning to the first sentence, using the word given. **Do not change the word given**. You must use between **two** and **five** words, including the word given. Here is an example (**0**).

0 When I was younger I wasn't allowed to eat ice cream before dinner.
   FORBIDDEN
   When I was younger, I was ...FORBIDDEN FROM... eating ice cream before dinner.
1 I used to run, but I stopped about six months ago.
   UP
   I .... about six months ago.
2 My dad asked: 'Are you going out on Saturday?'
   KNOW
   My dad wanted .... going out on Saturday.
3 I thought that film was going to be a lot more interesting than it was.
   NEARLY
   That film .... interesting as I'd thought it would be.
4 I didn't have my bank card on me, so I couldn't buy the boots.
   HAVE
   If I'd had my bank card on me, I .... the boots.
5 This is the most beautiful beach I've ever been to!
   SUCH
   I've .... a beautiful beach!
6 I'm always disappointed when the teacher gives me low marks.
   WHEN
   I always find it .... low marks by the teacher.

Vocabulary

Buying and selling

1 Choose the correct word to complete each sentence.

1 I don't care which **brand** / **company** of trainers I buy, as long as they are comfortable.
2 My new computer had a **trouble** / **fault** but as it was under guarantee, the company replaced it.
3 I love this store – the clothes are good quality and the prices are so **competitive** / **budget**!
4 When I got the jeans home, I found they didn't fit, so I took them back and **transferred** / **exchanged** them for a different size.
5 As soon as the new video game **appeared** / **presented** in the shops, it sold out.
6 I love **checking** / **browsing** around the arts and crafts market in my town.
7 My favourite coffee shop is just about to **launch** / **establish** a new flavour, which I can't wait to try.
8 It's important for companies to listen to what **audiences** / **consumers** say about their products.
9 My sister is brilliant at shopping. She always finds great **bargains** / **trades**, but I never do.
10 You should always check items carefully before you **invest** / **purchase** them to make sure nothing is wrong with them.
11 The sunglasses you want are out of **stock** / **sale** at the moment. Try again in a couple of weeks.
12 The department store in town has an amazing range of products on **offer** / **supply**.

People and feelings

2 Use these clues to help you find 15 words for feelings in the puzzle. The first letter of each word is given to help you. The words in the puzzle may go in any direction, including diagonally and backwards.

How do you feel in these situations?

1 You're watching a sitcom and it's making you laugh. **A** ....
2 You're amazed at the story your friend is telling you. **A** ....
3 You thought the test was this afternoon, but your friend says it's on Monday. **C** ....
4 Your little brother broke your phone. **F** ....
5 The bus leaves in two minutes and you're not at the bus stop yet. **A** ....
6 You made a silly mistake in front of your friends.
   F ....
7 You're bored, lonely and a bit sad. **M** ....
8 You've just begun a new hobby and you absolutely love it. **P** ....
9 Your cousin got a new bike and you didn't.
   J ....
10 You're well prepared for your test today.
   C ....
11 You're really hopeful about the future.
   O ....
12 You're so scared you can't move. **P** ....
13 You don't think enough is being done to protect the environment. **C** ....
14 You have made up your mind that you are going to win the cycle race. **D** ....
15 Your grandmother told you she dislikes the clothes you're wearing. **O** ....

A	G	H	I	O	C	Y	F	H	W	N	D	F	C	E
K	S	F	S	G	H	U	L	D	M	E	V	P	O	L
C	P	T	M	I	R	S	U	O	I	X	N	A	N	B
U	O	E	O	I	L	L	L	F	C	E	A	L	F	A
A	P	N	O	N	U	O	I	A	T	J	K	C	U	R
U	D	U	F	H	I	R	O	A	L	E	Q	V	S	E
Z	S	E	M	I	T	S	N	F	N	T	T	S	E	S
F	O	X	T	E	D	O	H	M	Q	Z	Z	C	D	I
Z	D	R	P	E	I	E	J	E	A	L	O	U	S	M
A	V	P	P	S	R	E	N	F	D	H	I	L	M	R
A	M	U	S	E	D	M	N	T	S	V	G	G	F	O
Y	N	A	C	I	T	S	I	M	I	T	P	O	F	M
E	P	C	O	N	C	E	R	N	E	D	E	A	Q	L
D	E	D	N	E	F	F	O	W	E	L	T	W	F	R
I	P	G	A	T	D	P	U	E	G	D	N	G	H	E

Writing

Part 2

A review

1 Read the review of Camden Market in London, and put the paragraphs in the most logical order.

Camden Market

A

It is situated beside Regent's Canal, and actually consists of a series of markets, each selling something different. You can get jewellery, clothing, books, antiques, items for the home, and lots more. In addition, there are more food stalls here than you can count, selling delicious dishes from every part of the world. Some of these places have outdoor seating with a view of the canal.

B

One thing to be aware of is that the market is very popular and can get terribly busy. If crowds are not your thing, then this might not be the place for you. Otherwise, I cannot recommend it highly enough. Just remember to take plenty of money with you!

C

London is a fantastic city for markets, and Camden is definitely one of the best. I've been several times and I never get tired of it. It's fun and colourful, and a great place to visit once you have had enough of the art galleries and expensive stores in other parts of the city.

2 What is the writer's main aim in each paragraph? Match each paragraph with one of the functions below.

1 expressing personal opinion
2 making recommendations
3 giving a factual description

3 Put the words in order to make sentences. Then match each sentence with a function from Exercise 2.

1 It's / time / not / here / wasting / worth / your / .
2 I / that / recommend / go / you / strongly / .
3 It / the / was / whole / on / alright / .
4 The / very / helpful / are / staff / .
5 It / at / a / prices / good / of / range / shoes / reasonable / sells / .
6 There / everything / signposted / two floors, / and / clearly / are / is.
7 The / badly / rooms / lit / are / small / changing / and / .
8 I / well-designed / place / the / that / has / been / feel / .

4 It's good to add emphasis when writing a review. One way to do this is to use adverbs. Choose the best adverb to complete each phrase.

1 It's .... worth a visit.
   well / greatly
2 It was .... amazing.
   strongly / absolutely
3 I found it .... interesting.
   incredibly / largely
4 The place was .... overcrowded.
   completely / deeply
5 The actors performed ....
   considerably / brilliantly
6 The course was .... helpful.
   extraordinarily / highly

5 Read the exam task below. Underline the three content points you are asked to write about and make some notes on each one. Then think about the facts and opinions you want to include.

> We are looking for reviews of local department stores. Your review should include information about where the department store is, what sort of things it sells and what the staff are like. Would you recommend the department store to other young shoppers?

✓ Exam task

Write your review. Don't forget to add a title, and to include a recommendation in your final paragraph.

Need help? Go to Writing bank page 100 in the Student's Book

Reading and Use of English

Part 3

1 Make adjectives from the words below using these suffixes: *-ive, -ful, -less, -able* and these prefixes: *in-, il-, im-, un-*. As well as adding the suffix or prefix, make any other spelling changes needed. Sometimes it is possible to make more than one adjective.

> acceptable   aware   convenient   decorate
> desire   doubt   end   extend   harm   legal
> patient   polite   prefer   skill   visible   willing

2 Make nouns from the following words. The changes don't require a suffix or prefix.

> advise   believe   grow   high   long   prove
> proud   see   strong   wide

3 Make *-ly* adverbs from the following words. Think carefully about spelling changes. Sometimes you will need to change the word into an adjective before you can add *-ly.*

> automatic   admit   comfort   continue
> drama   enthusiasm   expect   finance
> happy   necessary   passion   primary   ready
> science   success   surprise   suspicion

Need help? Go to Exam tips page 67 in the Student's Book

✓ Exam task

For questions **1–8**, read the text below. Use the word given in capitals at the end of some of the lines to form a word that fits in the gap **in the same line**. There is an example at the beginning (**0**).

Example: 0 CREATIVE

Space origami

The **(0)** .... art of paper folding, known as origami, is   **CREATE**
most **(1)** .... linked with   **CLOSE**
Japan, although the practice actually has roots in many cultures. It involves folding paper into a sculpture, without cutting or gluing it. Most of us have tried it. We've followed a set of **(2)** .... and felt   **INSTRUCT**
a great sense of pride and **(3)** .... on seeing a 3D   **SATISFY**
bird or frog emerge from a flat sheet of paper. Now, however, this skill that we learn as little children is **(4)** ....   **INCREASE**
being used by space scientists who need to find **(5)** .... ways of getting   **EFFECT**
large objects such as telescopes into space. The **(6)** ....   **DISCOVER**
they've made is that by folding them up, it's possible to fit them into a tiny space on top of a rocket.
When the object arrives at its destination, it's able to unfold robotically. The **(7)** ....   **PRESENT**
of a human astronaut isn't required. With this technique, projects that once looked **(8)** .... have now   **POSSIBLE**
become achievable.

Listening

Need help? Go to Exam tip page 69 in the Student's Book

✓ Exam task

🔊 **09** You will hear people talking in eight different situations. For questions **1–8**, choose the best answer (**A**, **B** or **C**).

1 You hear two students talking about a school project.
   Why is the girl annoyed?
   A She's not interested in the topic.
   B It will take her a long time to complete.
   C She'd prefer to work on it independently.

2 You hear a young person talking about his work.
   How does he feel about his success?
   A Grateful for all the help that he has had.
   B Surprised at the position he finds himself in.
   C Worried that he has made some bad choices.

3 You hear two friends talking about a display of winter lights in their local park.
   What is the boy's opinion of the display?
   A It's not worth the expense.
   B Little effort went into creating it.
   C Its popularity spoils the experience.

4 You hear a critic talking about a film.
   What does he say about it?
   A It's unlike any other film he has ever seen.
   B He doesn't share other critics' views of it.
   C There are people he wouldn't recommend it to.

5 You hear a football coach talking about picking players for her team.
   What is she mainly looking for?
   A good ball skills
   B a high level of fitness
   C the ability to work well with others

6 You hear a student talking to his teacher about a picture for an art competition.
   What is the student worried about?
   A how likely he is to meet the deadline
   B how quickly he can think of a title
   C how well he can fix a mistake

7 You hear a girl talking about her new part-time job.
   Where does she work?
   A in people's gardens
   B in a plant shop
   C in a park

8 You hear a boy talking about a school trip.
   What does he say about it?
   A He was disappointed with the choice of location.
   B He's not sure it was entirely successful.
   C He found it completely exhausting.

Vocabulary

Computers

1 Complete the compound nouns with the words from the box, then match each one with the correct definition.

> access   board   drive   engine   engineer
> networking   operator   reality

1 software ....
2 hard ....
3 computer ....
4 virtual ....
5 social ....
6 search ....
7 message ....
8 internet ....

a a program that helps us find information we need
b someone who manages computer systems
c the use of websites to connect with others
d the ability to get online
e a device that stores data
f a webpage where users can post and react to comments on a topic
g a person who writers computer programs
h computer-generated simulations of the world that users can interact with

2 Combine the words to make new computer words.

1 back ———————— put
2 book   load
3 down ———————— up
4 broad   base
5 data   sheet
6 spread   band
7 un   do
8 in   mark

Science

3 Match the words with the definitions.

> laser   microphone   monitor   satellite
> telescope   thermometer

1 This piece of equipment is sent into space, and it sends information back to Earth.
2 You use this piece of equipment to record sound.
3 This machine produces a very strong beam of light.
4 Scientists use this to see things that are far away.
5 This piece of equipment measures how hot or cold something is.
6 This part of your computer contains the screen.

Grammar
Relative clauses

1 Match the two halves of the sentences.

1 I've got a neighbour
2 I bought this T-shirt in the shop
3 At the music festival we had to camp in a field
4 I think I've lost the sunglasses
5 I wish I could remember the name of the boy
6 This is a picture of the hotel
7 I think the ocean scientist
8 The planet Mars is
9 Lots of money can be made by celebrities
10 There's a beach near me

a where scientists plan to send humans next.
b whose dog barks all day long.
c which had a sale last month.
d whose work I admire most is Sylvia Earle.
e where you can often find pretty shells.
f which my dad gave me for my birthday.
g who promote products online.
h where we bumped into Timothée Chalamet!
i which was miles from the stage.
j who I met at the party.

2 In which sentences from Exercise 1 can the relative pronoun be replaced by *that*?

3 Rewrite each pair of sentences to make a single sentence with a non-defining relative clause in the middle of it. The first one has been done for you.

1 NASA was founded in 1955. It's an American agency responsible for space research and aeronautics.
NASA, which is an American agency responsible for space research and aeronautics, was founded in 1955.

2 The NASA website is updated regularly. I love it.
3 Chris Hadfield spent 166 days in space. He's famous for playing the guitar on the space station.
4 The international space station is 420 kilometres above the Earth. Many science experiments are done on the space station.
5 The photos of space on the NASA website are amazing. They are very colourful.
6 There's a podcast about the history of space. I plan to listen to it.
7 The international space station has housed astronauts since 2000. It requires a crew of seven.

Writing

Part 1 Essay

1 Read the exam task. How many points must you include in your answer?

2 Read the answer and decide if the writer agrees or disagrees with the statement. What was the writer's 'own idea'? What do you think about the writer's view?

☑ Exam task

You must answer this question. Write your answer in **140 – 190** words in an appropriate style on the separate answer sheet.

In your English class you have been talking about the impact the internet has had on the world. Now your teacher has asked you to write an essay for homework.

Write your essay using **all** the notes and giving reasons for your point of view.
'Relying on the internet is making us all lazy.'
Do you agree?

> **Notes**
> Write about:
> 1. email
> 2. education
> 3. .... (your own idea)

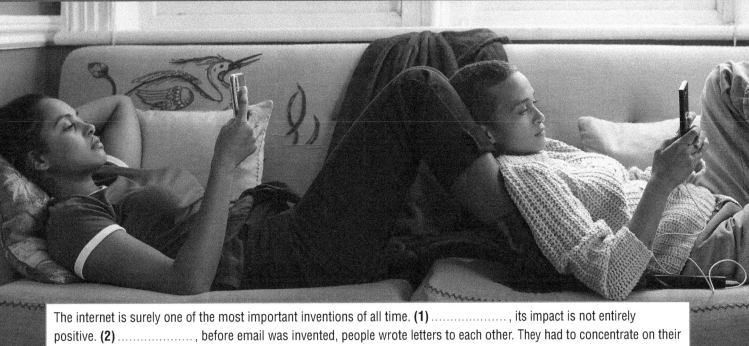

The internet is surely one of the most important inventions of all time. **(1)** ...., its impact is not entirely positive. **(2)** ...., before email was invented, people wrote letters to each other. They had to concentrate on their handwriting and actually walk to the post box to send their mail. This involved far more thought and effort than quickly typing an email and pressing send.

(3) .... we consider education, the problem is even worse. **(4)** .... looking information up in books, students can now use a search engine to find out anything they want at the click of a button.

(5) ...., they don't need to think for themselves so much any more.

(6) .... the internet is making us lazy is online shopping. **(7)** .... it is very easy to shop from your living room, when items arrive, they are often unsuitable for one reason or another. By putting in a little more effort, and actually going to the shops in person, such problems could be avoided.

3 Complete the answer with the words and phrases from the box.

Although   Another way   As a result   For example   However   If   Instead of

4 Look at this advice for answering the essay question. What has the writer done well, and what is missing?

- Write in paragraphs.
- Make sure each paragraph develops one idea.
- Use linkers to connect your ideas.
- Include three points – two you are given and one of your own.

- Avoid using informal language.
- Use pronouns like *it*, *this*, *these*, etc.
- Have a conclusion at the end.

5 Which would be the best conclusion to this essay, and why?

> **A** To sum up, I agree that the internet is making us lazy, but I understand that the modern world could not function without it. Therefore, we must find a way to use it sensibly, and not rely on it too much.

> **B** In my opinion, laziness is not a reason to stop using the internet. It has improved all our lives enormously, and the world would be a much worse place if we did not have it.

6 Write an answer to the exam task on page 34. Use these notes.

> **Notes**
> Write about:
> 1. entertainment
> 2. friendships
> 3. .... (your own idea)

Need help? Go to Writing bank page 96 in the Student's Book

Vocabulary extra

1 My community

1 Use the clues to complete the crossword with words about celebrations.

Across

2 A public celebration where people wear special clothes and dance and play music in the streets.

3 A line of people or vehicles that moves through a public place as a way of celebrating an occasion.

4 To come together with lots of people in a group.

5 A set of clothes that belongs to a certain period, person or country.

7 Something that makes a place look attractive.

Down

1 A custom that has existed for a long time.

6 A formal party that is given to celebrate a special event such as a wedding.

2 Complete each sentence with the correct form of the verb from the box.

> break (x2)   cheat   keep   look   make
> pick   put   rely   stick

1 It's really important for families to .... together when times are hard.

2 The weather was awful, so I had to .... the promise I made to take my little brother to the park.

3 When famous couples .... on each other, the media loves to print the details.

4 My uncle is a well-known scientist and I really .... up to him.

5 The children in Hayley's class sometimes .... fun of her because she's obsessed with cats.

6 The old lady next door gets lonely so sometimes I sit with her and .... her company.

7 The football coach tends to .... on Harry, but it's only because he doesn't try very hard.

8 Everyone felt shy at the beginning of the lesson, but the teacher played some games that .... the ice.

9 My parents are fantastic. I can always .... on them to give me great advice.

10 My little sister can be a nuisance, but I .... up with her behaviour because I love her.

3 Choose the correct word to complete each sentence.

1 Barbara and Suzanna are twins and have a very close **bond** / **contact** with each other.

2 My **number** / **circle** of friends hasn't really changed since I was at primary school.

3 There's usually a certain amount of **tension** / **harmony** in every family at some point.

4 Liam had a very interesting **upbringing** / **breeding**, as his parents travelled around the world while he was young.

5 No one knew each other at the party, so my dad had to make a lot of **meetings** / **introductions**.

6 I enjoyed the trip abroad but I found the **division** / **separation** from my family quite hard.

2 Home and away

1 Choose the correct word to complete each sentence.

1 Our flight was cancelled at the **final** / **last** minute, which was incredibly disappointing.
2 The journey involved a long ocean **voyage** / **trip**, followed by a trek through thick jungle.
3 The train arrived late and so we missed our **connection** / **association**.
4 Mount Fuji is truly an amazing **vision** / **sight**.
5 The expedition leaders accidentally took the group into dangerous **ground** / **territory**.

2 Choose the correct verb to complete the phrasal verbs. You may need to change the form of the verb.

| catch   get   head   keep   make   pull   see   stop   turn |

1 When my sister went abroad to study, we all went to the airport to .... her off.
2 On our way to New York, we .... over in Iceland for a few days.
3 The tour guide walked quickly and one elderly man found it hard to .... up with the group.
4 As we were driving through town, I asked Dad to .... over so I could get a drink from the shop.
5 My mum said she really needed to .... away, so Dad booked a short holiday for all of us.
6 'Go on ahead,' my sister said. 'I'll .... up with you all later.'
7 After visiting the mountains, we .... towards the beach.
8 The explorers were reluctant to .... back, but they were forced to by the weather.
9 As soon as we had collected our suitcases, we .... for the exit.

3 Complete the sentences with a word or phrase from the box.

| community spirit   housing estate   inner city   outskirts
picturesque   public spaces   residential   suburb |

1 Life can be hard for young people growing up in .... areas.
2 These days you find a lot of shopping centres on the .... of cities.
3 Neighbourhood life and .... are often strong in villages.
4 There are many wonderfully .... villages in the Swiss Alps.
5 A big new .... is being built on farmland to the north of my village.
6 My uncle lives in a .... of Beijing, but works in the city.
7 Cities need lots of .... such as parks where people can interact and have fun.
8 The most popular .... areas in cities are usually very expensive.

3 Performance

1 Complete each gap with the correct form of the phrasal verb from the box.

> get across   identify with   make out
> sell out   soak up   stand out

1 I liked the film, but it was difficult to ....
   what the characters were saying half the time.
2 Tickets for that musical you want to see have almost
   ....! We'd better buy some today.
3 The actor who really .... in that movie
   was Willem Dafoe. He was amazing.
4 My friend and I had a great time at the festival –
   singing, dancing and .... the atmosphere.
5 I really .... the main character. I could
   totally see his point of view.
6 The message the film was trying to ....
   was that it's important for people to be kind to
   each other.

2a Read the text, ignoring the gaps for now. Put the sections into the correct order. The first one has been done for you.

1 ...E....   4 ....
2 ....   5 ....
3 ....   6 ....

2b Now complete the text using the words from the box.

> appearances   approval   crew   edits   location
> outline   promote   publicity   streaming

3 Choose the correct word to complete each sentence.

> beat   charts   choir   goes   lyrics
> rhythm   solo   track

1 I can't sing well enough to join a ....
2 I can't remember how that song ....
3 I love dancing to music that has a strong
   ....
4 Do you think the pop .... matter
   any more?
5 This is my favourite .... on the album!
6 The .... of this song are very moving.
7 Jane sang two verses .... before
   everyone joined in.
8 My dad has no sense of .... at all.

The stages involved in making a film

A

Finally, once the release date of the movie is known, the actors will make **(1)** .... on TV to further **(2)** .... the film.

B

During production, filming will take place. The director works with the cast and film **(3)** .... to ensure everything goes according to plan.

C

In the pre-production phase, the script will be finalised, the cast and crew will be hired, a budget will be set, and a **(4)** .... chosen.

D

The next phase is distribution. Deals are made with cinemas and **(5)** .... services to show the film.

E

The development stage involves coming up with an idea and getting **(6)** .... to go ahead. Then, the writers must create an **(7)** .... of the plot.

F

Post-production is when the director reviews and **(8)** .... the footage and adds in the special effects, sound and music. It's also when the trailer is made. A **(9)** .... campaign to increase awareness of the film will be organised at the same time.

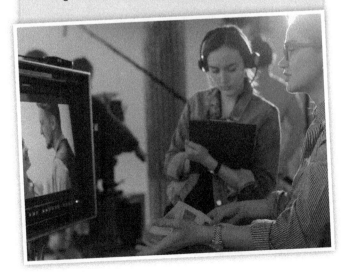

Fit and healthy

1 Match a word from box A with one from box B to form sport expressions. Use each word only once.

A

> competitive   football   represent
> save   set   shoot   victory   win

B

> a goal   a record   at a target   lap   pitch
> sports   the trophy   your country

2 Now complete the sentences with expressions from Exercise 1. Make any changes necessary.

1 It's incredible! I don't know how he managed to .... that .... ! The ball should be in the back of the net.
2 Sir Mo Farah .... the first world .... of his career in 2020, at the age of 37.
3 After completing the 100 m final, the winner did a .... in celebration.
4 It's a very special thing to be asked to .... at the Olympics.
5 The .... was in poor condition before the start of the match.
6 In archery, competitors must .... arrows ....
7 The rest of my family enjoy .... like tennis, but I prefer things you do alone, like aerobics and hiking.
8 When their team finally .... , the fans went wild.

3 Match the words with the definitions.

1 condition   a a person trained to prepare or sell medicines
2 eyesight   b a sensation or change in your body that is associated with a disease
3 pharmacist   c a natural substance that your body needs to keep it healthy
4 remedy   d you do this often when you have a cold
5 sneeze   e an illness or medical problem
6 symptom   f this is what you use to see
7 vitamin   g a medicine or therapy that helps make you better
8 wound   h an open injury on the body

4 For each group of words, circle the odd one out and explain why it does not fit the group. The first one has been done for you.

1 dairy ⟨portion⟩ protein   vegetables   carbohydrate   Portion is the odd one out. The rest are food groups.
2 peel   chew   swallow   taste   bite   ....
3 aubergine   cherry   leek   sour   crab   ....
4 mild   rich   salty   starving   tough   ....
5 bun   loaf   toast   roll   pudding   ....
6 rotten   off   bad   ripe   stale   ....

5 Lessons learnt

1 For each verb, circle the word or phrase that does <u>not</u> collocate with it.

1 **achieve**   a goal   success   excellence   an objective   a result   an idea
2 **reach**   your potential   the limit   an agreement   a conclusion   an opportunity
     a decision
3 **gain**   experience   a chance   access   control   a fortune   support
4 **fail**   in an attempt   to mention   to qualify   in concentration   to convince
     to persuade someone
5 **miss**   a target   your potential   an error   the point   the chance   an opportunity

2 Complete each sentence with a preposition from the box.

> beyond   for   from (x2)   in (x2)   of   to (x3)

1 The two company founders were locked in a struggle .... power.
2 After my brother graduated .... university, he got a job in finance.
3 It's a fantastic feeling when you succeed .... doing a new task for the first time.
4 The teacher didn't like my project as she said I had failed .... provide enough analysis.
5 Once I had progressed .... beginner level, I started to really enjoy playing the piano.
6 For some people, it's hard to decide what subject to specialise .... at university.
7 Someone in my class was suspended .... school for cheating in a test.
8 After I read the introduction .... the book, I knew I'd enjoy it.
9 Vulcanology is the branch .... geology that deals with volcanoes and related processes.
10 My cousin has applied for admission .... medical school.

3 Choose the correct word to complete each sentence.

1 Modern teaching techniques make **knowing** / **learning** a lot more fun than it used to be.
2 My dad is a highly **educated** / **informed** person but even he could not understand the instructions.
3 Some teachers are better than others at maintaining **discipline** / **punishment**.
4 The academic **levels** / **standards** at my school are quite high.
5 My brother was sad when his job application was **resisted** / **rejected**, but he's trying again.
6 It's really important to get the proper **training** / **studies** before you teach young children.
7 I'm nervous as I am **sitting** / **getting** my first English exam tomorrow.
8 Some scientists have done a **research** / **study** on the effects of early-morning lessons on teenagers.

6 Our planet

1

Complete the puzzle with the missing words in these sentences. The first letter is given to help you. What word is revealed in the grey column?

```
1  [ ][ ][ ][ ][ ][ ]
2  [ ][ ][ ][ ][ ][ ][ ][ ]
3  [ ][ ][ ][ ][ ]
   4  [ ][ ][ ][ ][ ][ ]
   5  [ ][ ][ ][ ]
6  [ ][ ][ ][ ]
      7  [ ][ ][ ][ ][ ][ ][ ]
   8  [ ][ ][ ][ ][ ][ ]
      9  [ ][ ][ ][ ][ ][ ]
10 [ ][ ][ ][ ][ ][ ][ ][ ][ ]
```

1 In my family we try to eat only **o** .... food as far as possible.

2 A strong **e** .... can cause buildings to fall down.

3 The weather will be **s** .... tonight, with heavy rain and lightning.

4 Bananas are grown in **t** .... regions of the world.

5 We visited a fantastic nature **r** .... at the weekend.

6 I do my best to keep my carbon **f** .... as small as possible.

7 There are many **c** .... in cleaning products that are not good for us.

8 Companies are good at making their products appear **g** .... when they aren't really.

9 Seeds can remain in the **g** .... for many years before they germinate.

10 **C** .... efforts have helped save many species from extinction.

2

Change each word using suffixes and/or prefixes so that it completes the phrase on the same line.

1 danger   an .... species
2 ecology   .... problems
3 extinct   mass ....
4 coast   .... villages
5 environment   an .... disaster
6 global   a .... protected species
7 region   on a .... basis
8 new   a .... resource
9 biology   .... functions

3

Match each animal word with the correct definition.

| bark feathers habitat leopard owl |
| paw swan territory trap wasp |

1 the noise a dog makes ....
2 a bird is covered in these ....
3 the area a wild animal controls ....
4 a thing that is used to catch wild animals ....
5 the foot of an animal such as a bear ....
6 a type of wild cat that has spots ....
7 a bird with a very long neck ....
8 a yellow-and-black flying insect ....
9 a bird with very large eyes ....
10 the natural environment of a plant or animal ....

7 Influences

1a Complete the table with the abstract nouns.

Adjective	Abstract noun
1 certain	....
2 desperate	....
3 dissatisfied	....
4 impatient	....
5 passionate	....
6 relieved	....
7 suspicious	....
8 sympathetic	....

1b Complete each sentence with an abstract noun from the table.

1 The talk was boring but I tried hard not to show my .... with the speaker.
2 I wish my friend had shown a bit of .... instead of laughing when I fell off my bike.
3 Photography is a .... of mine.
4 It's clear that the main character in the story only steals out of ....
5 I knew with absolute .... that my parents wouldn't let me go to the party.
6 I felt a huge sense of .... when I heard I had passed my music exam.
7 .... amongst voters could see the government lose the election.
8 I had a .... that my brother had taken my tennis racket.

2 Complete the sentences by choosing the correct word from the box.

> breath   death   ears   face   fool   heart   mood   nerves   spirits   temper

1 My friend's chattering sometimes really gets on my ....
2 I could not believe my .... when my sister told me she was engaged.
3 The beauty of the view took my .... away.
4 Dad was in high .... yesterday because he got a promotion at work.
5 My brother's in a .... and won't talk to any of us.
6 The film shows that it's possible to recover from a broken ....
7 I'm sorry, I just can't .... going out tonight.
8 I didn't mean to, but I lost my .... when we lost the match.
9 I was so happy I Jumped around and made a bit of a .... of myself.
10 I didn't really enjoy the film – it scared me to .... to be honest!

3 Match the two halves of the sentences.

1 I waited beside the counter for ages
2 It's hard to keep up with fashions
3 It was a horrible moment
4 Prices are very low here
5 My new debit card is really useful
6 I was really upset to learn

a as it is accepted in most shops and restaurants.
b before anyone came to take my money.
c that the video game my cousin wanted was temporarily unavailable.
d when brands bring out new designs so often.
e because they are selling old stock to make space for new collections.
f when I realised I had left my shopping on the bus.

8 Breakthrough

1 Complete each sentence with a noun from the box.

> breakthrough   cure   discovery   evidence
> observations   progress   scale
> statistics   study   theory

1 There is very strong .... now that eating sugar is bad for you.
2 Researchers carried out a .... that showed how important our social lives are to our health.
3 According to the latest .... , crime rates in the city are coming down.
4 By making careful .... , astronomers could work out the position of the comet.
5 Scientists have achieved a major .... in their understanding of global heating.
6 I recently read an article about a new .... of how gravity works.
7 The .... of antibiotic drugs meant doctors were able to save many lives.
8 It seems impossible that there will ever be a .... for the common cold.
9 The huge .... of the problem of deforestation isn't properly understood by the public.
10 The experiment is in .... now and the results will be ready in two years.

2 Choose the best verb for each gap.

1 The biologist .... the creature carefully.
  A examined   **B** experimented   **C** explored
2 It's difficult to .... how fast populations will grow.
  A define   **B** conduct   **C** estimate
3 Scientists want to .... their new theory as soon as possible.
  A estimate   **B** test   **C** determine
4 The first thing the doctor did was .... the patient's height and weight.
  A measure   **B** research   **C** survey
5 It's important to .... all the possible causes of the fire.
  A calculate   **B** investigate   **C** inspect
6 The researchers will .... the impact of the recent flooding.
  A assess   **B** count   **C** decide

3 Match each phrasal verb in bold with the correct paraphrase below.

> constitute   made clear   performed
> proposed   thought of   were discovered

1 An experiment was **carried out** into the effect of exercise on the body.
2 The young researcher **came up with** a great way to study the problem.
3 The biologist **pointed out** that the research was unfinished.
4 Unfortunately, the results **turned out** to be unreliable.
5 It's sad that girls **make up** a small proportion of all engineers.
6 Scientists **put forward** the suggestion that we should all eat less meat.

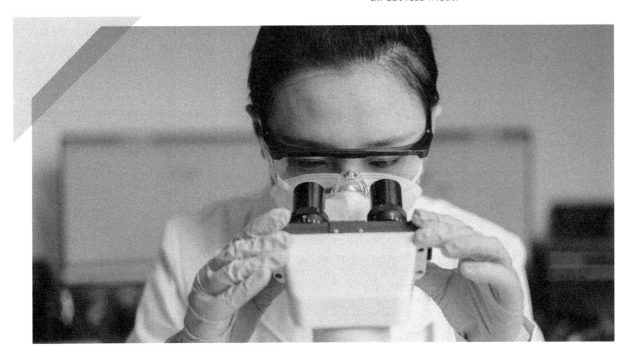

Audio scripts

You will hear five short extracts in which teenagers are talking about making new friends. For questions 1–5, choose from the list (A–H) what each speaker says. Use the letters only once. There are three extra letters which you do not need to use.

Speaker 1

I've had lots of practice at making new friends! Because of my dad's job, we had to move to a new city every two years. It was tough; I'm not going to pretend it wasn't. Those first few days at a new school I was always nervous. But luckily, I'm an outgoing person and I enjoy building up a new social circle. One thing to realise though – the worst thing you can do is try to rush things. Just be patient – let the process take its course. Also, remember that people will always be curious about someone new. Don't take offence at annoying questions – just smile and be polite.

Speaker 2

When I was little, it was so easy to make a new friend. I just went up to someone I liked and said, 'Do you want to be my friend?' Nine times out of ten, they said yes and off we went! Once you get to secondary school it doesn't work quite like that. In that environment you need to act cool – give the impression that you're completely at ease, no matter what's going on inside. That way, people will find you interesting and want to learn more about you. You'll get asked to do stuff with them outside school and from there you'll be friends in no time.

Speaker 3

I think making new friends is quite hard. I know there are people who can just strike up a conversation with a stranger, and straight away they're laughing and joking together, as if they've known each other for years. But for the rest of us it takes a bit more effort. If I find myself chatting to someone that I'd like to be better friends with, I'll try and point out something I know we both enjoy – it might be a sport we both do, or the fact that we're both good at art, that sort of thing. A shared love of something is the root of a good friendship, I think.

Speaker 4

The temptation when you're trying to make new friends is to really go for it – make loads of jokes, get everyone laughing, generally make yourself seem as interesting as possible. This can have the opposite effect to the one you're after, though. What you want to do is let people see the true you. Answer questions honestly and be as natural as you can. Joining clubs is quite a good thing to do, too. Sometimes it's easier to talk when you're both busy doing something – it gets rid of those awkward silences, which can be really uncomfortable.

Speaker 5

One thing that separates an acquaintance from a friend is that as well as having fun together, friends support each other through the tough times. Offering to be there for someone is a great way to build a stronger relationship. It doesn't have to be anything emotional – it could just be that you are both entered into a race, for example, and you have some good tips on how to train and what you should be eating. The thought of doing this might make you feel a bit nervous, but it really shouldn't.

You will hear people talking in six different situations. For questions 1–6, choose the best answer (A, B or C).

1 *You hear a boy talking about a computer course he did during his summer holiday.*

Boy: My dad found out about it, and booked me onto it. I'm not sure how he heard about it. He's really keen for me not to waste my time during the holidays. I try to explain to him, and Mum does too, that it's OK to chill out a bit once in a while, but he's not having it. I wasn't against the idea, to be fair, even though it did eat into my free time quite a bit. But I picked up a lot of stuff that I didn't know, and the tutors managed to make it challenging and interactive.

2 *You hear two friends talking about a podcast series.*

Girl: Thanks for telling me about that podcast series. I listened to an episode last night and it was just as funny as you said it would be.

Boy: They're great, those presenters, aren't they? It doesn't matter what they're talking about – I just love the way they are together.

Girl: The episode I chose was the history of biscuits. I'm not sure how much time they actually spoke about that, though!

Boy: Not much, I imagine! Try the one on ballpoint pens. Honestly, you won't regret it!

Girl: If you say so!

3 *You hear a report on the radio about an expedition.*

Reporter: This month a team of adventurers from Britain will first climb, and then cycle down one of the world's highest mountains. Exactly which one is yet to be revealed, but it will be over 7,000 metres high. The idea is to raise money for community projects that enable young people aged from 12 to 18 to get involved in adventurous sport. You can support the project by visiting the expedition website and donating online. You can also find biographies of the adventurers, and technical details about all their gear.

4 *You hear a girl talking to her father about a problem she's got.*

Girl: I asked a teacher about borrowing a laptop, Dad, but none are available.

Father: Well, you'll have to carry on using mine for the moment.

Girl: Yours is so old and slow. What did the guy at the repair shop say about mine?

Father: He still hasn't got back to me, actually.

Girl: But it's been two weeks. Surely they'd have had time to look at it by now?

Father: I'll pop in tomorrow after work and see what I can find out.

Girl: I bet they'll say it needs replacing. We should have got a new one as soon as it broke!

5 *You hear a teenager talking to his grandmother about his recent move.*

Grandmother: How are you settling in to your new home, Tom? What do you think of the town?

Tom: It's interesting, Gran, nothing like where we were before. Not as many people of course – but everything we need is right here. I mean school, the doctor, the shops, the train station. Honestly, it takes no more than ten minutes from our house to get to all of those. There are lots of cycle paths as well, so getting around is a piece of cake. I miss my friends though, and the places we used to go to together. It doesn't quite feel like home yet.

Grandmother: Early days! You've not been there very long.

6 *You hear part of a class debate.*

Teacher: OK, what a great debate we're having! It's fantastic to get all your views on the new statue they are putting up in our town square. Now, does anyone want to add anything? Oh yes – Julie. Go ahead, what would you like to say?

Julie: I honestly don't see what everyone is going on about. We want more tourists to visit our town, don't we? Well, in that case we've got to make improvements. The square was so bare and boring before. Fair enough, this statue might not be to everyone's taste, but you're never going to please everyone.

🔊 04 Unit 3, Listening Part 4

You will hear an interview with a teenager called Alice Fields, who runs a film club at her school. For questions 1–7, choose the best answer (A, B or C).

Interviewer: My guest today is Alice Fields, a student at Treeway High School. Last year Alice started a film club for students at her school and it's been a huge success. In fact, two members have won national awards for film reviews they've written. Alice, tell us what inspired you to start your club.

Alice: Well, I'm obsessed with films – I want to work in the film industry when I'm older. But when I chatted to my friends about it, none of them seemed to get it. I felt they were missing out, so I just thought – how can I get them to have the same enthusiasm for it that I have? And starting a film club seemed one way to do that.

Interviewer: And how did you go about setting up the club?

Alice: Well, I had to see if the Head Teacher would let me do it first. Students don't normally run clubs at my school so there was no set procedure. Initially it was 'Oh no, that's so complicated! We don't know what to do about that!' But I stuck at it, and eventually they agreed. Then I persuaded a friend to help me get it going. We did some advertising around the school and slowly but surely students started to sign up.

Interviewer: And how much staff involvement is there now?

Alice: We have a teacher who observes, but that's it – the running of the club is down to us. But hardly a week goes by when a teacher doesn't drop in to see what we're watching or have a chat with me about a film I've advertised on a club poster. In fact, I'm now looking into opening up the club to staff as well as pupils – I've got a feeling there's enough interest.

Interviewer: Tell me what happens on a typical club night.

Alice: Well, we watch the film of course, and then we either have a follow-up discussion on the themes, or I run a session on review writing. But the main thing is the film. I want to get that sense of being in a cinema. I set out the seats in rows, I bring popcorn, I show trailers, all that! But I do expect people to behave well. I have rules on what's acceptable and what's not, and I remind people of them when needed.

Interviewer: What do you enjoy about running your film club?

Alice: So many things! One is witnessing friendships grow between people who had previously never spoken to each other. It doesn't seem to matter if one is 11 and the other is 14 – as soon as they realise that they both love the same type of film, they've got that thing in common with each other and they never look back.

Interviewer: Now, what about those members of yours who won awards for their film reviews? How do you teach them to write good reviews?

Alice: So, when I coach the club on writing reviews, I talk a lot about the six essential elements of film: the three Cs, which are: colour, camera, character, and the three Ss, which are: story, setting, and sound. I remind students to think about these elements in turn and that usually prompts ideas. I also tell them not to be afraid to say things that lots of people will disagree with. After all, you've got to grab the reader's attention somehow.

Interviewer: And finally, what advice would you give to someone thinking of starting up a film club of their own?

Alice: Oh – go for it! The benefits are huge, honestly – but do be prepared for the hard work! Things to bear in mind – stick to the same day and time every week, otherwise attendance will drop. Assign roles to students as this encourages a sense of ownership. Also – don't have an age barrier, and finally avoid putting any pressure on people to go each week. Just let them dip in and out as they please.

Interviewer: Fantastic! Thanks, Alice …

🔊 05 Unit 4, Listening Part 2

You will hear a teenager called Louise Porter giving a class presentation about a water sport called paddle boarding. For questions 1–10, complete the sentences with a word or short phrase.

Louise: Morning, everyone! In my presentation today I'm going to talk about my favourite sport – paddle boarding. It's a sport that has its roots in surfing. To do it, you stand up on a board that floats on the water, and move yourself along using a long stick with a broad, flat end, called a paddle.

The idea of standing on a board and using a stick to move yourself along isn't new, of course. When I was doing my research for this presentation, I found out that for thousands of years, cultures from Africa, South America and Asia did this for the purposes of fishing, travelling and even, surprisingly, having fun, which I thought was brilliant!

In its modern form, paddle boarding's been part of the water sports scene for about 20 years, but its popularity really took off about five years ago. My family and I first tried it two years ago and I can tell you it's currently the world's fastest growing sport.

It's not hard to see why. For one thing, paddle boarding's a great way to get fit. You have to use all your major muscle groups, and it gives your heart and lungs a workout, but at the same time it's quite gentle. This suits people who for whatever reason aren't into tough, energetic workouts.

What it's also got going for it is that it is so straightforward to learn – nothing like as hard as learning to ride a bike, for example. One thing I'd say though, is that it's really important to learn how to swim before you go paddle boarding, if you can't do it already.

Another attraction of paddle boarding is that it lets you get really close to nature. We paddle board in the sea near our home, and there's so much wildlife to see. I've always got my eyes open in case I spot a dolphin or a porpoise, and just last weekend a seal jumped onto my paddle board. It gave me such a fright! But it soon realised my board wasn't a rock after all, and slipped back into the water.

I love paddle boarding on rivers too. You can see a lot more from a paddle board than from, say, a canoe or a kayak. You're standing up, for one thing, so you have a much better view. Also, you can look down into the water from a paddle board. From a kayak, the reflections usually make that impossible.

What's great about paddle boarding is that it's so easy to mix with other activities. My mum does yoga on hers – it sounds crazy, but I'm going to have a go soon, and I can't wait. For my dad, it's all about using the board to go birdwatching. I go with him now and again and it's quite fun – but perhaps a bit too slow and quiet for me.

To make it easier to do different things on your paddle board, it's possible these days to get a board that you can attach things to, such as a picnic box, or a chair. I've seen some that you can add a motor to, but for me, that's going a step too far!

When it comes to buying a paddle board, there are so many types available, depending on what you are going to use it for. Ours are the inflatable kind that you blow up using a pump. The great thing about these, compared to solid ones, is that they fit in a backpack and you can carry them easily. You don't need a special rack on the car or anything like that.

You must be wondering if there are any negatives at all to this sport. Well, not many, actually! We go out onto the water all year round, even in the winter, when it's freezing cold. The only thing that puts me off is if it's a really windy day. But other than that, we make sure we have the right clothes and equipment and just get on with it!

You will hear a man called Paul Mathers talking about a summer technology camp for teenagers. For questions 1–10, complete the sentences with a word or short phrase.

Paul: Hello, everyone! My name's Paul and it's great to see so many of you here for my talk. As you know, I'm going to tell you all about Teencoders summer camps. These are a fun way to learn computer programming through projects such as 3D game design, laser printing and loads more. It's a fascinating topic and one that's so important in our modern world.

Our courses run throughout August, and are held at a beautiful location called Helmsely College. Accommodation is in single bedrooms and there's one bathroom for every four students. Our residential campers usually stay for a week. They arrive on Sunday night and leave on Friday afternoon. People who live nearby can come as a day camper.

For students who wish to stay for longer, we offer something we call a 'bridge weekend'. It's very reasonably priced and covers food, accommodation and fun activities, including a cinema trip, from Friday afternoon until the new campers arrive on Sunday evening.

So let me tell you about the daily schedule. Campers wake up around 8.00 a.m. and breakfast is available between 8.15 and 8.45. Day campers are expected to turn up no later than 9.00, ready for everyone to start sessions at 9.30. Typically, there are five sessions a day with an hour-long break for lunch at 1.00. The sessions end at 5.30.

After dinner, residential campers choose from a range of evening activities, such as laser tag, or chocolate making. This year for the first time we're adding electronic art to that list, so it'll be interesting to see how popular that is. Campers can also choose to play board games or use the time for relaxation.

So, what are some of the things you can learn on this course? Well, as you know, the tech world moves incredibly quickly, and we make a huge effort to keep up. Virtual reality has come on massively over the past few years, so that features in our courses, but of course we also cover basic programming principles. You won't get far without that.

For the first hour of the day, we present students with a puzzle. We find this gets people's brains into the right place for the rest of the day's learning, and also helps settle everyone down. Students love it and say the time flies by much quicker than it does in a normal lesson.

After that there's a morning lecture. We call it that, but that makes it sound terribly serious. In fact, groups are small enough that everyone can ask questions whenever they like. It's very informal but lots of new material is presented so concentration is essential.

In the afternoons, you get to put what you have learnt into practice. For instance, we might get you to design a smart home device. Actually doing stuff is a great way of learning. Reading about how someone else designed a video game, for example, just won't be as effective.

Our tutors are all amazing and the teenagers who come on our courses rate them very highly indeed. We employ university students who are all aiming for careers in technology. Some of our former tutors are data scientists now, and sometimes we invite them in to run sessions on technology careers.

So, we really hope to see you at a camp soon. Have a word with your parents tonight. They needn't worry about you. We promise to send them email updates every day on your activities and progress. It's a great way to keep in touch as we don't allow mobile phones on the course!

You will hear an interview with a young blogger called Emma, who's talking about living a 'zero-waste' life. For questions 1–7, choose the best answer (A, B or C).

Interviewer: Hello, everyone and welcome to this week's podcast. I'm very pleased to have with me in the studio today teen blogger Emma Jackson. Emma, tell us a bit about zero-waste blogging.

Emma: Well, it's really catching on! Some people who do it have become really famous. For those who don't know, the zero-waste movement's all about cutting the amount of waste you produce to an absolute minimum. The most famous zero-waste bloggers, the ones who started the whole thing off, produce just a jam jar's worth of waste a year, which really is quite incredible! I admire them, but that's not possible for me. I just try to live, as far as possible, without generating too much rubbish.

Interviewer: I know some people have a problem with the term zero-waste. What about you?

Emma: It's something we're stuck with, I think. But it does give people who disagree with us something to attack with, which is unfortunate. I've read loads of articles saying that because we do throw some stuff away, we are cheats and liars. If we could say we're low-wasters for example, that would solve a lot of problems. And, of course, no one can ever actually get to 100 percent zero waste, so it's not the most accurate way of describing what we do.

Interviewer: So, Emma, have you always had a good attitude towards waste?

Emma: I'm afraid not! It's been a slow process. My dad has always been really into environmental issues and nature and all that, and you'd think this would have influenced me – and I guess it did have an effect eventually, given what I do now. But when I was little and my parents tried to get me to put rubbish in the right recycling bin, I really couldn't be bothered.

Interviewer: Like all of us, I guess! Now I've heard about a neighbourhood survey you did. Tell me about that.

Emma: It was something we did for our geography class. We had to write a survey, and go out and collect information on our neighbours' recycling habits and how they felt about waste, that kind of thing. It really opened my eyes to just how much stuff we throw away unnecessarily and I slowly started to think about my own behaviour.

Interviewer: So, what was the first thing you did?

Emma: I stopped using plastic drinking straws. It's not something that's going to change the world, I know that, and it's kind of embarrassing to say really, now that I have gone so much further. But it got me onto the right track mentally, to go on and do bigger things. Gradually after that, I did more; I became aware of people on social media, read some really inspiring stories, and it just flowed from there really.

Interviewer: So, give us some tips. What would you say to someone who's just starting out?

Emma: Well, it's funny, people start trying to live a zero-waste life and they look around their home and all they can see is plastic stuff – toothbrushes, hair brushes, clothes hangers, you name it. The temptation is to immediately throw out all this perfectly good stuff and go out and get eco-friendly ones made of wood or metal. That's not a good idea though – make sure you use whatever you have until it comes to the end of its life. Then by all means, get the eco-catalogue out and treat yourself!

Interviewer: That's great advice, Emma. I'm sure there are lots of mistakes people make. Any last words of advice on that?

Emma: Yes, be realistic. Mistakes are fine, accidents are normal. I've been known to go out on a hot day without my reusable water bottle and then I have to get a plastic bottle of water from a store. Or I leave my fabric napkin at home and need to use paper ones. I am angry with myself, sure, and I try not to do it too often. But none of us are perfect, we're just humans trying to do our best. That's how I look at it.

You will hear five short extracts in which teenagers are talking about going shopping. For questions 1–5, choose from the list (A–H) what each speaker says about going shopping with friends. Use the letters only once. There are three extra letters which you do not need to use.

Speaker 1

Not everybody likes going clothes shopping with friends. Some people find the whole thing a real bore and just want to get into the shop and out of it as fast as they can. For me, it depends a lot on what I want to buy. If it's something fairly routine like a pair of jeans, I'm happy to have company. I know I'm not going to hold people up, or drive them crazy with my inability to make a decision. But if I'm feeling adventurous and want to explore shops I've never been to, then I'd rather do that by myself.

Speaker 2

I definitely prefer shopping with friends to shopping alone, especially if I need something quite urgently. On my own, I seem to get distracted really easily – I might need a top for a party that evening for example, and yet somehow I find myself wandering around shoe shops, or looking at sportswear. And the other thing is mistakes – friends have stopped me more than once from buying something on impulse that I would most likely have regretted, and then had to return. I'm not saying I always listen to what they say – I do have my own opinions too – but often I'm glad they were there!

Speaker 3

I love clothes shopping, but at the moment I'm on a tight budget – I'm saving up for a new skateboard, so I'm not buying new stuff. I do still go shopping with my mates though. It's an important part of how we socialise. We have a lot of fun, trying on different things, discussing the latest trends and giving each other advice. Shopping together brings us closer as a group for sure. It's interesting because we all have different styles, so it's surprising that it works so well. I guess we're in tune with each other's tastes, so we naturally take that into account when we give each other advice.

Speaker 4

Most of the time I shop alone. I seem to get more done in a shorter amount of time. But my best friend Holly and I are good shopping partners. We don't get impatient if one of us takes forever in a particular store – but at the same time we don't drag the other one into stores we know they hate. I love shopping for jewellery, for example, but Holly hates it. So while I do that she might spend time looking at make-up, or just have a coffee. I've got several friends I refuse to go shopping with – it sounds awful but I'd just rather go by myself.

Speaker 5

If you're the type of person that's really confident about their style, then you probably don't need anyone else's input, and you probably don't need to go shopping with other people. But if you're like me, someone who appreciates a bit of support and advice, then you will. I suppose you could ask the shop assistant, but when it's a friend, you trust that person and they know you and your tastes well. My friends often come up with ideas for outfits that would never occur to me. They open my eyes to possibilities that I wouldn't see otherwise.

🔊 **09** **Unit 8, Listening Part 1**

You will hear people talking in eight different situations. For questions 1–8, choose the best answer (A, B or C).

1 *You hear two students talking about a school project.*

Boy: The geography project sounds like it's going to be a lot of work, doesn't it?

Girl: It really does! But at least the teacher's given us a couple of months to do it. That takes the pressure off a bit. I just wish we didn't have to do it with a partner – I get on much better on my own.

Boy: You are funny! I don't mind that, but I wasn't sure about the topic. Is there that much to say about flooding?

Girl: Well, yeah. It's getting to be a real problem in some parts of the world, isn't it?

2 *You hear a young person talking about his work.*

Boy: My grandma looked after me a lot when I was growing up because my parents worked long hours. She taught me to bake, and my favourite thing to make was cupcakes. It was when I was about 15 that I started selling them, and the business just grew from there. Now I'm 18 and I've got employees, my own factory … I'm not quite sure how it happened. It's not what I imagined I'd be doing as a career but I've got no plans to stop just yet. In the long term though, I imagine I will move on to something else.

3 *You hear two friends talking about a display of winter lights in their local park.*

Boy: I went to see the lights in the park last night.

Girl: Oh, what did you think of them? I haven't been, as Mum says the ticket price is ridiculous.

Boy: It is, to be honest. I mean, it does look amazing – there are lights through all the trees, along the paths and on the buildings. But the whole thing is over in 30 minutes and you're not given a chance to really appreciate it – there are staff all along the route encouraging you to keep moving.

Girl: I'd hate that. Is it because there are lots of people there?

Boy: I've heard it can get crowded, but it wasn't when we were there.

4 *You hear a critic talking about a film.*

Critic: I wasn't expecting much when I went to see this one – the reviews that have come out in the press so far didn't fill me with confidence. But I adored it. It almost felt like I'd seen a different film from the one I'd read about. I laughed at all the jokes – well there were a few that I didn't understand, but that could be to do with my age! The film is aimed at young people, there's no denying that. But my advice is – don't let that put you off. It's great.

5 *You hear a football coach talking about picking players for her team.*

Coach: Lots of students want to get onto the school football team and they just can't understand why they're not being picked. They show me fancy things they can do with the ball, bouncing it from knee to head and that sort of thing, and demonstrate good communication on the pitch – all of which is great of course. But if they get out of breath after 15 minutes, that's no good, and I see a lot of that. So that's the area I'm concentrating on at the moment, in my selections.

6 *You hear a student talking to his teacher about a picture for an art competition.*

Teacher: Your painting looks great, Greg! Do you think you can finish it by this evening? That's when you need to deliver it to the town hall for the judging, isn't it?

Greg: That's right – shouldn't be a problem. It's finished really, but I need to deal with this section here, where I accidentally painted over a really important figure. I'm not sure I can get it back to how it was. It's such a shame.

Teacher: Just take your time, it'll be fine. What are you going to call the painting?

Greg: I've got no idea to be honest. Something will come to me at the last minute, it usually does!

7 *You hear a girl talking about her new part-time job.*

Girl: I'm surprised how much I enjoy my new job to be honest. I have to get up really early, that's the only thing I don't like. But I've noticed that I'm getting fitter and stronger – it's all the manual work, I guess. I love being outdoors all day, even when it rains and I get all muddy. I have made a couple of mistakes. I pulled out some bushes one day that I thought were dead, but apparently they weren't. The home-owner wasn't too pleased about that!

8 *You hear a boy talking about a school trip.*

Boy: I've never been on a school trip like that one. We did so many different things – and actually often didn't really have enough time to get the most out of each one. I could have spent a lot longer at the beach to be honest, and a bit less time at the museum. But I'm not complaining. It was such a relief to get out of the classroom for a while and do something a bit different. Some of the kids were really tired at the end – I'm not sure everyone enjoyed it that much.

Acknowledgements

The authors and publishers acknowledge the following sources of copyright material and are grateful for the permissions granted. While every effort has been made, it has not always been possible to identify the sources of all the material used, or to trace all copyright holders. If any omissions are brought to our notice, we will be happy to include the appropriate acknowledgements on reprinting and in the next update to the digital edition, as applicable.

Key: U = Unit

Text

U4: The Guardian for the text adapted from 'Manchester United's Katie Zelem: 'Italy changed me as a player – and a person'' by Louisehttps://www.theguardian.com/profile/matthew-cantor Taylor, *The Guardian*, 23.04.2021. Copyright © 2022 Guardian News & Media Limited. Reproduced with permission; **U6:** Omar Tello for the text on 'Omar Tello, a hero of the environment. Reproduced with kind permission.

Photos

All the photos are sourced from Getty Images.

U1: Maskot; Klaus Mellenthin/Westend61; Klaus Vedfelt/DigitalVision; Borja B. Hojas/Getty Images News; **U2:** Â© Marco Bottigelli/Moment; by wildestanimal/Moment; TravelCouples/Moment; **U3:** Bet_Noire/iStock/Getty Images Plus; Hill Street Studios/DigitalVision; gorodenkoff/iStock/Getty Images Plus; **U4:** John Peters/Manchester United; A-Digit/DigitalVision Vectors; Jamie Grill Photography/Tetra images; **U5:** Prostock-Studio/iStock/Getty Images Plus; SDI Productions/E+; skynesher/E+; **U6:** Michael H/DigitalVision; Auscape/Universal Images Group; Mark A Paulda/Moment; Maskot; **U7:** RgStudio/E+; Richard Newstead/Moment; RgStudio/E+; **U8:** Erik Simonsen/Photodisc; Klaus Vedfelt/DigitalVision; sinology/Moment.

Cover photography by DisobeyArt/iStock/Getty Images Plus.

Animations

Grammar animation Video production by QBS Learnings. Voiceover by Dan Strauss.

Audio

Audio production by Leon Chambers.

Typesetting

Typeset by Hyphen S.A.

URLs

The publisher has used its best endeavours to ensure that the URLs for external websites referred to in this book are correct and active at the time of going to press. However, the publisher has no responsibility for the websites and can make no guarantee that a site will remain live or that the content is or will remain appropriate.